CLEAR CONSCIENCE

The **ATOM BOMB** vs. . .

the **SUPER HOLOCAUST**

by *General Raymond Davis*
Medal of Honor – U.S. Marine Corps

and *Judge Dan Winn*
Senior Judge – State of Georgia
and U.S. Marine, WWII

FREE
Poster inside
Includes chron
of the war an
of the Pa

CLEAR CONSCIENCE

The ATOM BOMB
vs. the SUPER HOLOCAUST

by
General Raymond Davis (Ret.)
Medal of Honor – U.S. Marine Corps
Assistant Commandant U.S. Marine Corps

and
Judge Dan Winn
Senior Judge – State of Georgia
and U.S. Marine, WWII

Turner Publishing Company
Paducah, Kentucky

Published by:

Turner Publishing Company
412 Broadway
P.O. Box 3101
Paducah, KY 42002-3101

Publisher's Editor: Bill Schiller

Photo credits
Front cover: left, © National Atomic Museum; right, Alliance for Preserving the Truth of the
    Sino-Japanese War
Back cover: top right, © U.S. National Archives; middle, © Raymond Davis, bottom, ©Judge Dan Winn
Front cover flap: © Brig. General Paul W. Tibbets
Pgs. viii-ix: © Brig. General Paul W. Tibbets
Pgs. 24, 35-38, 57, 69: © U.S. National Archives
Pg. 132: © Judge Dan Winn
All other photos compliments of the Alliance for Preserving the Truth of the Sino-Japanese War
Poster: © U.S. National Archives and the Alliance for Preserving the Truth of the Sino-Japanese War,
    photo of Brig. General Paul W. Tibbets in front of Enola Gay, © Brig. General Paul W. Tibbets,
    Mushroom cloud © National Atomic Museum.

Book design by Shock Design, Inc.
Printed in the United States of America

03 02 01 00 99   5 4 3 2 1

Library of Congress Catalog Card Number: 99-61895

ISBN: 1-56311-445-3

Contents

DEDICATION

This book is dedicated from me to my wife, Knox Davis.

Ray Davis

DEDICATION

This book is dedicated from me to my deceased mother and fathers, Mary Peace Winn and Frank M. Winn; and to my deceased sister, Lt. Jean Winn (Weston) who served in the Navy WAVES during World War II. I believe she was the first officer candidate recruit from the state of Georgia.

Dan Winn

Foreword

I, along with all veterans of World War II, most all military personnel, and most informed Americans, was appalled at the anti-U.S.A., anti-military and anti-Truman display of the Enola Gay, proposed by the National Air and Space Museum of the Smithsonian Institution in 1995.

As Judge Dan Winn asked me to join him in presenting this book to the world in the hope that it will give a true historic perspective on the Atomic Bomb and its proper use by the United States of America, it is a pleasure to participate in this project.

From my experiences in Peleliu, and as we point out in the book, an invasion of Japan could have sacrificed almost the entire Marine Corps force, along with a large portion of our Navy and Army.

— General Raymond Davis (Ret.)
Medal of Honor – U.S. Marine Corps
Assistant Commandant U.S. Marine Corps

Prologue

For over 50 years I have been listening to the Japanese and many factually incorrect historians criticize President Harry Truman, the use of the Atomic Bomb, and me and my crew for dropping the Bomb on Hiroshima. The ongoing, near total distortion of history, along with the proposed Enola Gay Exhibit at the National Air and Space Museum, completed a blatantly incorrect picture favoring the Japanese propaganda campaign on the Bomb and the end of the war.

The crew of the *Enola Gay* before takeoff for Hiroshima
L to R standing:Lt. Col. John Porter, Capt. Theodore J. Van Kirk, Maj. Thomas W. Ferebee, Col. Paul W. Tibbets, Capt. Robert A. Lewis, and Lt. Jacob Beser
L to R kneeling: Sgt. Joseph Stiborik, SSgt. George R. Caron, Pfc. Richard H. Nelson, Sgt. Robert H. Shumard, and SSgt Wyatt Duzenbury.

I was delighted when Judge Dan Winn approached me about publishing a book revealing the many atrocities performed by the Japanese and the use of the Bomb to end a horribly barbaric war. This book is intended to counter those revisionists dominating the media and present a true historical account for present and future generations. What you are about to read will shock you, and it should. It is long overdue that these activities and statistics be revealed and included in our history books. Upon reading this, you will understand why President Truman and our country had no choice but to stop the Japanese as quickly as possible, and that included dropping the Bomb.

I repeat what I said in my book, *Flight of the Enola Gay:*

"On August 6, 1945 as the Enola Gay approached the Japanese city of Hiroshima, I fervently hoped for success in the first use of a nuclear type weapon. To me it meant putting an end to the fighting and the consequent loss of lives. In fact, I viewed my mission as one to save lives rather than to take them. The intervening years has brought me so many letters and personal contacts with individuals who maintain that they would not be alive today if it had not been for what I did. Likewise, I have been asked in letters and to my face if I was not conscience stricken for the loss of life I caused by dropping the first atomic bomb. To those who ask, I quickly reply, 'Not in the Least.'

That is still true."

After 53 years I still have a CLEAR CONSCIENCE about the Bomb, as I know President Truman did.

— Brigadier General Paul W. Tibbets
Pilot of the Enola Gay that dropped the
Atomic Bomb on Hiroshima in 1945

Introduction

In August of 1945, the United States of America used the Atomic Bomb to destroy the Japanese cities of Hiroshima and Nagasaki. Japan surrendered, thus ending the tragedy which has come to be known as World War II. The dropping of the bomb was one of the most important historical occurrences of all time.

The necessity, humanity and wisdom of President Harry Truman's decision to use the bomb has long been the subject of books, debates, discussions, and commentary on the part of the news media, academia, and citizenry in general. President Truman's position was that the bomb saved many lives, not only American lives, but lives of those in our Allied forces, lives in China and, yes, even the lives of Japanese civilians. Because so many lives would be spared from the horrific onslaught of a ground invasion, there was no better choice than the bomb. Veterans of the war and most people from that generation know this to be true. Somehow, that knowledge, in itself, will not prevail historically if we are to give credence to those who constantly distort and destroy what could otherwise be regarded as plain and simple TRUTH.

For over 50 years now, servicemen from that era which prepared for the invasion, have resented the revisionist claim that their millions of lives were expendable. They resent any notion that their lives were less valuable than the city of Hiroshima or Nagasaki.
Therefore, this book serves as an answer to these simple questions:

1. Would the Japanese have surrendered without the bomb?
    Conclusive evidence is that they would not.

2. Did the Bomb save more lives than it took?
    It spared more lives, well into the millions.

3. Should we have doubts about the Bomb being correct?
    We should have no doubts, but live with an absolute clear conscience.

In a secretly intercepted communication among the Japanese high command, Foreign Minister Mamoru Shigemitsu embarked on a campaign of what he referred to as "propaganda" to immediately discredit use of the bomb. The purpose of this propaganda was to divert attention from Japan's horrendous treatment to prisoners of war as well as their merciless killing rampage through China and Asia which had taken place for decades.

For over 50 years, every August 6th, there is a highly publicized visit to Hiroshima by the Japan leadership. The event is headed by the Emperor and there is much deploring of the use of the Bomb. The United States is referred to as "barbaric". And though there have been many excellent articles and books which support the use of the Bomb, the historical correctness of that action has been somewhat overshadowed by the incessant depiction of Hiroshima victims and seeming endorsement of the Japanese view that it was not necessary. Tragically, some have made a totally unacceptable comparison of it to the Holocaust.

This anti-American slant on the use of the Bomb has, in fact, been furthered by some of our own anti-bomb theorists. I was very disturbed to watch a televised documentary of the war which was hosted by ABC's Peter Jennings. It appeared his sympathy was fully aligned with the Japanese. My research also led me to one particular book wherein the authors (Lifton & Mitchell) claimed that the Bomb "has weighed heavily on our national conscience" and that we have a "raw nerve" over Hiroshima. The authors stated that this country has been in "fifty years of denial". The book was extremely caustic and unfair in its criticism of President Harry Truman. The authors maintained that the Bomb has "eluded reasoned discussion". The natural explanation for this is that nine out of ten programs by a mis-informed media have been anti-nuclear in content. There has never been anything resembling a debate format relative to the bomb.

Even so, the vast majority of Americans approved of the A-Bomb. They accepted the President's statement that it was correct given the treacherous attack on Pearl Harbor which launched our involvement into World War II. Many have said that America was justified in ending the war with the bomb. The propaganda still continues though, and this revisionism reached a crescendo during the time of the proposed Enola Gay exhibit at the National Air and Space Museum which was to commemorate the end of WWII in the Pacific. The exhibit, in the heart of the Smithsonian Institution at our nation's Capitol, was orchestrated by some wild politically correct professors (headed by Martin Harwitt) who lacked real insight into the reasons for the use of the Bomb. They lacked reasonable analysis for its use, but seemed to have an anti-nuclear agenda.

These distasteful and flawed narrations of distorted history have caused me and others who care about true historical accounting to speak out with our views on the subject. This book, in part, serves as a challenge to those like Harwitt, Jennings, Lifton and Mitchell in the hope that they would participate in a national forum with us and participate in "a reasoned discussion" on both sides of the A-Bomb issue. Beyond this, it should be known that a feeling of resentment has been building up within us veterans... a feeling which would have been best reflected in the original title for this book- "Shut Up About the Damn A-Bomb!"

The facts which follow are true and should be conveyed to every United States citizen and student who passes through their respective institution of higher learning. The use of the Atomic Bomb should never reflect adversely on the morality or humanity of the United States of America.

-Judge Dan Winn

Note: Throughout many historical accounts you will find the following spellings, Nanking and Nanjing, referring to the same city in China. I have recorded them here exactly as I found them in my research, therefore, you will find both spellings throughout this book.

Preface

The Enola Gay Crew — Today

There have been some intimations or rumors concerning the Enola Gay crew and particularly concerning their mental health as it related to memories of the dropping of the Atomic Bomb.

This author had the distinct privilege of attending a reunion of the 509th Composite Bomb Group in Dayton, Ohio recently. I had occasion at length and very closely, to associate with members of Brig. General Paul W. Tibbets, Jr.'s crew; Viz. Dutch Van Kirk, navigator; Tom Ferebee, bombardier; and Richard Nelson, radio operator.

This writer can say, without equivocation, that none of these members of the crew had the slightest indication of any negative residual mental feelings of any kind from the mission to drop the bomb.

They were as mentally alert and sharp as anyone could imagine and, Brig. General Paul W. Tibbets, Jr. was as sharp as anyone could imagine although being 84 years of age.

One could know in listening and talking to all of them, that they had the positive feeling of regret that the atomic bomb was necessary, but they had absolutely no regret that the bomb had been used.

In speaking with General Tibbets, the feeling was that he could not begin to entertain any feelings of remorse for dropping the bomb because before even thinking of that, he would think of the many Marines and many Army personnel who would be killed and maimed in an invasion of the homeland islands, and also the many Navy personnel and ships that would be sunk, and he would think of the Kamikaze planes that would have caused tremendous casualties both to the landing troops and the Navy . He would think of the airmen, his B-29 companions, who were beheaded years prior to the end of the war for simply being captured in Japan and the many airmen in all services who would be tortured and beheaded as the horrible war continued. He would also think of the many, many millions of civilians that would have been killed in an invasion of Japan, particularly as a great percentage of the civilian population was programmed to die in trying to inflict as much death as possible on the invading armies.

When this writer returned from the reunion in Dayton, I stopped by to see a childhood friend of mine, Al Fowler in Douglasville, GA. Al was a B-17 pilot and in the North African theater at about the same time General Tibbets and a good portion of his crew were also in North Africa in a B-17 squadron.

When we were discussing my trip to Dayton and my meeting with General Tibbets and his crew, one of the first things that Al asked me was how were they "getting along". He had read the rumors and innuendos about their having health problems and guilt feelings and some going crazy over thinking about their mission in dropping the bomb.

I was somewhat shocked at his really thinking this, as he had extensive bombing missions of his own in the European theater.

I assured him that any stories or rumors he had heard concerning any problems the Enola Gay crew may have had, were totally unfounded and that they were all as alert and mentally healthy as any people could be.

A quite interesting sequel to General Tibbets' career is the fact that his grandson, Capt. Paul Tibbets IV, became a B-2 Bomber pilot in 1997. Capt. Tibbets attended the Dayton Reunion and gave a very informative talk on the most sophisticated and expensive plane in the world.

— Judge Dan Winn

CHAPTER 1

Correct Decision

This book will show by uncontroverted facts that the decision by President Harry Truman to authorize the United States of America military personnel to drop the Atomic Bombs on Hiroshima, Japan August 6, 1945 and Nagasaki, Japan August 9, 1945 was, not only a 100% proper and correct military decision, but considering all the humanitarian and military circumstances at the time, it was mandated.

There should never be these little unfounded statements by latter-day revisionist historians that the use of the Atomic Bomb was even questionable. There was not then, or now, any reasonable argument against the use of the Atomic Bomb. It was absolutely, unequivocally, without question or doubt, the decision President Harry Truman should have made. He should be forever eulogized and credited with being a great leader.

There is no moral difference between the Atomic Bomb and any other bomb dropped on any city in World War II. No different than London, Manchester, Birmingham, Liverpool, Berlin, Hamburg, Cologne, Bremen, Shanghai, Nanking, or Manila. Only the magnitude of the bomb was different.

CHAPTER 2

Japanese Propaganda Motives

This book will also demonstrate how and why the Japanese leadership has used their glib, self-righteous, deprecating criticism of the Bomb for over 50 years to practically obliterate from recorded history their Imperial Army's Super Holocaust in killing some 30,000,000 civilian men, women, children and babies (far outnumbering Germany's Holocaust) in China, Southeast Asia and the Pacific, prior to and during World War II; including the most savage, inhuman rampage ever known on this earth. And that history included the most beastly conduct ever seen in war. Conduct too numerous for this chapter, but beginning with the indescribable torture of all of our fallen airmen, followed by the beheading of all of them. That hideous obscured conduct also included the order from the Japanese High Command to execute all of the 150,000 allied prisoners (and up to 300,000 more political and military prisoners and detainees of other countries) in the event of an invasion.

CHAPTER 3

A Short Chronology of War With Japan

T he United States was catapulted into World War II on December 7, 1941, after Japan, without warning, began bombing American naval vessels and military installations at Pearl Harbor in Honolulu, Hawaii. Among the vessels and aircraft that were destroyed were five battleships and literally thousands of United States military personnel and civilians.

The Japanese military forces, with direct approval of the Emperor and those in High Command, followed the Pearl Harbor bombing with some four years of the most atrocious, savage and in-human war crimes ever recorded in history.

This savagery occurred while the Japanese hordes enveloped China, Singapore, Hong Kong, Indo-China, in fact all of Southeast Asia, the Philippines and all Pacific Islands west of the Hawaiian Islands as well as those north of Australia.

Americans began many bloody, deadly, island-hopping campaigns throughout the entire Pacific Ocean and Southeast Asia which ended when the United States succeeded in capturing the Philippines and Okinawa. Suddenly, America and its Allies found themselves poised on the threshold of the most horrendous invasion that could be imagined. "Operation Downfall" was the code name given for a plan to invade the main islands of Japan.

Instead of launching this plan, some four years after Pearl Harbor (Aug. 6, 1945), the U.S. dropped the first Atomic Bomb on the city of Hiroshima, Japan; and on August 9, 1945, the second Atomic Bomb was dropped on Nagasaki, Japan. Approximately, 190,000 people were killed in the bombings and Japan surrendered August 15, 1945, bringing an abrupt end to World War II.

CHAPTER 4

Japan Prior to Pearl Harbor: Their Super Holocaust

In order to understand all of the history surrounding the war with Japan you must understand the Japanese empire prior to World War II.

For more than 50 years prior to World War II, the Japanese had not only occupied Korea, conscripted the men for military service, and enslaved its people, but had also committed untold atrocities against the Korean people, torturing, raping, killing Koreans and almost destroying the entire culture of Korea. They took Korean, Chinese, Malaysian and women of all occupied countries and distributed them as sex slaves, "comfort women", for soldiers in Japan's far-flung military machine. They had invaded China and used China as an experimental battle field, beginning about 1931, though actual war was not declared until 1937; after the fake Mukden Incident was used as an excuse to broaden the invasion of China.* Actually they used live Chinese people as a laboratory for inhuman tests, such as poison gas, medical experiments, germ and biological warfare experiments and plague infestation. (See Chapter 8, Unit 731).

A poorly equipped China, at that time, was subjected to invasion and killings and, as hard as it is to imagine, the total atrocities inflicted on the Chinese vastly outnumbered the atrocities committed by Nazi Germans. (More on this Super Holocaust in a later chapter).

The Japanese gloss over their atrocities during the decades prior to World War II with an occasional "broad apology" for their "conduct in Asia"; never for the atrocities in Nanking, all of China and, in the Philippines during the early stages of the war, nor for the atrocities in the Philippines. These were more horrible than the initial atrocities where some 70,000 or so Philippine troops were captured on Bataan and annihilated. They slaughtered some 100,000 Filipinos as they were losing the Philippines in the later stages of the war.

Neither have they ever admitted nor talked about the horrible Bataan Death March killing thousands of Americans, and, above all, the manner in which they treated the Americans before they killed them. (In another portion of this book it is pointed out that these same savage military soldiers were later designated, honored and enshrined, as kami, or gods, in the Yasukuni Shrine in Tokyo for having been one of those who brought peace to Japan). The Japanese never, in their history books, specifically point out the millions slaughtered by their military in the name of "opposing colonization" by other countries.

---

*The Mukden incident occurred on September 18, 1931 when a Japanese secret agent planted a bomb under a Japanese owned train. The subsequent explosion gave Japan a justifiable excuse to broaden the war and occupy all of Manchuria

In connection with the Japanese claim of occupying the countries of Asia and the Pacific because of western colonization, anyone interested should talk with Koreans of the period, Chinese of that period, Malaysians, Singapore citizens, Indonesian citizens and many small and large islands they occupied.

Those people who lived through the Japanese occupation could give historians a most enlightened account of that occupation and the fact that it had nothing to do with western imperialism. Those countries were conquered only for the tremendous ruthless expansionist ambitions of the Japanese.

It is shocking to see the Japanese distort their history so as to never acknowledge the past horrible military history in which they were cruel conquerors of many nations, many islands and many people. Nowhere in their history books, or in current accounts circulating in Japan, do they recognize any of the atrocities occurring in China, Korea and Southeast Asia, or the Philippines or the Bataan Death March.

Particularly, they of course want to forget, and do not record the proper perspective on Pearl Harbor as being a treacherous sneak attack in which the United States of America was a total victim to the extent of the killing of thousands of Americans and the destruction of a large part of our Navy.

It is continually shocking to see intelligent people who are supposedly knowledgeable about modern history who have a distorted idea of war history, and much other history, because the propagandists, mainly the Japanese, are promoting their agenda.

It is almost impossible to find a correct history of the Japanese expansion in all of Asia and China, except in a very few books which

I will point out later in this book. That history has been, so far as the Japanese are concerned, **totally obliterated**.

Search all your encyclopedias, reference books, and history books and you will find no account of the atrocious actions of the Japanese Imperial Army. I have a book on major events of the 20th Century and not a line about the vicious era concerning the Japanese Imperial Army: Where are these historically correct professors when history is not only being distorted, but being totally obliterated?

Most Japanese probably want the truth, but the belligerent Samurai, Knights of Bushido extremists are similar to the minority of Germans, the extremists, who claim that the Holocaust never actually happened. There has been a question in the minds of many as to the aggressive agenda of the Jewish people in promoting continuous displays, museums and exhibits concerning the Holocaust.

But in looking at the distortion of other history, it is easy to see that the Holocaust can be and is being totally distorted by a radical few trying to control the history of the ages. It must be kept in perspective as to why the Jewish people are consumed with the idea of making sure mankind never forgets the Holocaust.

The same principle should apply to Japanese history. We will reiterate many times that we are now friends of the Japanese, we want to continue to be friends of the Japanese, however we will not sit idly by and allow the history of the years prior to World War II, the Japanese domination of tremendous portions of China and much of Asia, and their Super Holocaust, to be obliterated for the sole purpose of giving validity to a distorted historic argument about our use of the Atomic Bomb, and whether it was appropriate.

CHAPTER 5

Rebutting Continued Historical Distortions

In the face of so many distorted historical accounts, Retired Air Force Brigadier General Paul W. Tibbets has had to defend himself, President Truman and the crew of Enola Gay in dropping the Atomic Bomb. He needs and deserves complete support from all Americans.

Many Americans continue to be duped by these historical accounts and have some wild, weird sense of over-analyzing the use of the Bomb. This book is written in anger over such things as the Hiroshima documentary on Public Television May 27, 1996, which contained material that would make any military person, or any correct thinking person who had read any of the true history of the war, almost sick.

It would make any member of the Armed Services who served in the Pacific during World War II actually sick; along with the millions of military personnel and their families who were being transferred from the horrible war in Europe to face another killing field in which they might have a 50% chance of survival. The ones in the initial landings would have much shorter odds than that.

There were songs and eulogies to the dead and injured of Hiroshima. The Chronicler stated that Americans were left with a raw nerve over Hiroshima; that we have a nuclear entrapment feeling, that we have denial over the use of the Bomb; and that we need to be liberated from our nuclear entrapment.

This is truly nauseating.

On this program, there was a reading of a maudlin speech by an American, Celeste Holmes, quoting the pitiful victims; showing endless pictures of victims. The final irony on the program was that the Mayor Hiraoka had stated in a very condescending manner that we would have to "wait for history" to judge whether the bomb should have been dropped.

We do not need to wait for history which is being totally molded and warped by pitiful people using some weird philosophy to distort the true history of the war, and the true history behind the atrocious Japanese military war machine, which had dominated China and Asia for decades.

Instead of asking questions about President Truman and the Atomic Bomb, Americans should be answering all of the questions. Who produced that Public TV program? The Japanese Foreign Ministry? Or the same people who flock to the Yasukuni Shrine?

(See page 115).

Public television should produce another program to let some clear thinking Americans present the proper perspective on the Bomb and why we have no reason to have a 'raw nerve' or feel "nuclear entrapment."

On a great number of occasions since August 1945, the wisdom of President Harry Truman ordering the use of the Atomic Bombs has been called into question by the Japanese, of course. Or by someone else too ignorant to know or examine the facts surrounding its use. Criticism of President Truman and the United States of America (I should emphasize that the United States of America used the bomb, and that it was in behalf of the United States of America) seemed to intensify during the many 50 year commemoration programs or projects concerning the end of World War II. The necessity and morality of the decision to use the Atomic Bomb to end the war was assailed by many in the United States. Many high officials in Japan used the 50 year commemoration ceremonies in Japan to try to brand the USA as barbaric.

Barbaric![1] How ironic: From a nation that, for over 50 years prior to Pearl Harbor had enslaved Korea, rampaged through China; murdering 30,000,000 people in China and Southeast Asia and tortured and murdered our military personnel in the Bataan Death March, after the capture of Corregidor, for no other reason than unbridled savagery.

---

[1] An unforgivable statistic for the Japanese: 45% of the American prisoners of war held in Japanese concentration camps died, while only 2% or 3% of the prisoners in German concentration camps died. Barbaric?? The Japanese Military gave special attention to the torture and killing of American and other white prisoners.

As I will elaborate for you later, the Japanese military had been, and were at the time, the most inhuman military regime in all of history. Let me repeat; the Japanese military forces who rampaged, almost unchecked, through China, Southeast Asia and the Pacific in a Super Holocaust for decades prior to and including World War II, were the most inhuman, barbaric and destructive of human life, in all of history. All of history? Yes.[2]

In short, the Japanese have **no standing** to question the morality or brutality of the Atomic Bomb.

Do other countries have the right to question its use? Of course they do. They can question the use of the Atomic Bomb from a historical or humanitarian standpoint, and the whole purpose of this book is for other countries, now and through the ages, to know, and never to doubt, the correctness of the use of the Atomic Bomb in August of 1945.

---

[2] The Nazi Germany extinction of over 6,000,000 Jews in that Holocaust is the most unbelievably cruel barbaric and inhuman attempt at the elimination of a race of people in all history.

CHAPTER 6

Proposed Smithsonian Enola Gay Exhibit: A National Disgrace

The culmination of 50 years of propaganda concerning the Atomic Bomb (as opposed to the true recording of historic events involving millions of World War II deaths) occurred during the 50th Anniversary Exhibit to be placed in the National Air and Space Museum. The main part of the Exhibit was to be the Enola Gay, the B-29 Superfortress which dropped the first Atomic Bomb on Hiroshima, August 6, 1945. The title of the exhibit was to be "Crossroads: The End of World War II, the Atomic Bomb and the Origins of the Cold War". This exhibit, as proposed by the National Air and Space Museum, was to only show the nose-cone of the Enola Gay and was one of the most vile, repulsive, exhibits imaginable. It was a special insult to military personnel in all of World War II, and was an insult to the intelligence of the

American public; that is, except to the few wild idiots who, I feel, had no sense of correct history and that were headed by Martin O. Harwitt, the Director of the Smithsonian Air and Space Museum.

This exhibit was dominated by photographs of the suffering Japanese and the horrors of the Atomic Bomb dropped on Hiroshima and Nagasaki. (No one would argue with the immediate horror of these two bombs and at no time has the United States sought to diminish the awful destructive power of the bombs.) The glaring insults of the exhibit were spot-lighted by one of the worst phrases one could use about the Pacific War, and I quote: "For most Americans, this was a war of vengeance." "For most Japanese, it was a war to defend their unique culture against western imperialism".[3]

Historically, nothing could be further from the truth. Here is a country who started a war with a sneak attack on another country, (killing thousands of its military personnel and civilians), and who is depicted as only defending its "unique culture". A shocking revelation came from the curator of the exhibit, Michael J. Neufeld when he stated that a discussion of probable United States casualties during the proposed invasion of Japan or rather the eminent invasion of Japan, was not "historically relevant" to President Truman's decision to drop the bomb.

Now just let that sink in a moment. It does not matter how many Americans would die in an invasion, the Bomb to prevent it should not have been dropped, what deep thinkers we had at the National Air and Space Museum.

---

[3] If you followed this same reasoning, Hitler and the Nazis were only protecting their "unique culture" in killing 6,000,000 Jews. I wonder if Michael Heyman, Smithsonian Director, would have sat idly by and let that be part of an exhibit.

Very notable in the exhibit was the eulogizing of Kamikaze pilots, as being heroes. Kamikaze pilots who were so fanatical as to commit suicide by diving into American warships, in devotion to their Sun God Emperor, do not qualify as heroes, when they were totally indiscriminate, and who dove into a navy hospital ship the USS Solace, killing 6 nurses for the glory of Japan. What heroes! As a matter of fact the Kamikaze pilots were far from volunteers. They understood that if they refused they were disgraced. Being disgraced in the Japanese Imperial Army meant one thing: Sayonara Baby!

Eighty-one members of Congress expressed their total disagreement at the exhibit and tried to remind the Smithsonian of the charter: "The Smithsonian Institution shall commemorate and display the contributions made by the military forces of the nation toward creating, developing and maintaining a free peaceful and independent society and culture of the United States, the valor and sacrificial service of men and women of the armed forces shall be portrayed as an inspiration to the present and future generations." As expected, the Veterans of Foreign Wars and the American Legion and the Air Force Association were appalled at the proposed exhibit, and pointed out that the Japanese were depicted as victims, despite their decades of aggression, atrocities and brutalities against American and allied civilians and military personnel, and in spite of their history of having killed some 30,000,000 people in China, Southeast Asia and the Pacific Theater in a tremendous Asian and China Holocaust.

Another astounding occurrence was disclosed when it was revealed that no input had been asked from Veterans Associations, or from knowledgeable military historians concerning the exhibit, or from the

Air Force. It was shockingly disclosed that the Smithsonian National Air and Space Museum staff had "Federal Expressed" the script of the proposed exhibit asking for a quick response from the Japanese, seeking their input into the exhibit. Reprehensible, that it had been impossible to have input from any of the American military organizations in the exhibit; and that the Museum staff would seek Japanese input. The Japanese had no right to dictate any of the terms of this exhibit.

The Veterans of Foreign Wars, American Legion, Air Force Association and also a 6 member review team composed as follows: Brigadier General William M. Constantine, USAF (Ret.), volunteer NASM Docent and Team Chairman; Colonel Thomas Alison, USAF (Ret.), NASM Curator for Military Aviation; Dr. Gregg Herken, Historian and Chairman, NASM Department of Space History; Colonel Donald Lopez, USAF (Ret.), former NASM Deputy Director and Senior Advisor Emeritus; Kenneth Robert, NASM volunteer Docent; and Dr. Steven Soter, Special Assistant to the Director, NASM and Team Secretary, attempted to work out a reasonable solution for the presentation of the exhibit that would be fair historically. But after considerable review by the knowledgeable review team and also after several exhibit changes, Martin Harwit continued to be arbitrary.

Director Martin Harwit, Director of the National Air and Space Museum arbitrarily fixed 63,000 as the maximum casualty loss which he would put in the exhibit as the number of Allied casualties anticipated in the event of an invasion of Japan, to compare against the casualties in the Hiroshima and Nagasaki bombs. As opposed to the 63,000 which he would finally agree to put, after negotiation; they had originally stated in the proposed exhibit that the Allies would only have 25,000 casualties in an invasion of Japan. How BIZARRE!

Although the Veterans of Foreign Wars, American Legion and Air Force Association were continually willing to work in good faith to make the exhibit historically correct, the Smithsonian, rather than reach any reasonable compromises on the exhibit, canceled the exhibit January 30, 1995.

If any part of this book indicates the Bomb was probably dropped for vengeance, you're reading it wrong. If you think it was dropped in punishment, you're wrong. All accounts of Japanese atrocities in this book are to show why they are trying to and have, put guilt darts toward us. Also to show they have no standing to criticize the Bomb.

The brainless wonders at the National Air and Space Museum must have had some deep-seeded dislike for American military personnel or American Armed Services, to want to form this exhibit into some pasquinade directed at those military personnel who so mercifully ended the war; led by a great President, Harry Truman.

How dare these people entrusted with our National Air and Space Museum take it upon themselves to try to anathematize President Harry Truman, and all the others who had a part in that glorious event.

Brigadier General Paul Tibbets, Jr. (retired) and all the others who rode with them, should not have to defend that event every August 6th. We ought to lead a memorial service for and with them, each August 6th and we should insulate them from criticism by our entire populace proclaiming that what they did was correct, and approved, and have none of this garbage each year, adding to the questioning of the decision to drop the Bomb. The Enola Gay should be enshrined (in full) in the National Air and Space Museum with commentary by appropriate patriotic Americans selected by Congress and not by some politically correct morons masquerading as intellectuals.

Why should servicemen and citizens of our World War II era and those who went through the Pacific War have to listen to this blather each August, and why would all of the World War II veterans and for that matter, Veterans of all of our wars, have to wonder why any American would be more concerned with the people who died at Hiroshima or Nagasaki than the hundreds of thousands of his buddies who were casualties in the Pacific; and useless casualties at that? And why would we have to be wondering why Americans, or any other countries, would be more concerned with the people who died at Hiroshima or Nagasaki than the additional millions who would have died in an invasion of Japan?

If accounts of World War II continue in the present direction, the Japanese will have future generations believing the Pearl Harbor sneak attack was a defensive maneuver to keep the United States fleet from entering Tokyo Bay; and that it was necessary to cripple or sink most of our Pacific fleet in the name of anti-colonialism. Have any accounts by the Japanese rulers, or Japanese historians, acknowledged that the sneak attack on Pearl Harbor was wrong or bad? They will occasionally, in a back-handed way, say they "regret the war in the Pacific". (Only because it brought destruction to their conquering military aspirations.)

This junk about the Japanese only being interested in fighting "to defend their **unique culture against western imperialism,**" when coming from an American, can only come from a warped mind which has distorted anti-nuclear feelings. All of us, with any common sense, have anti-nuclear feelings. The proper exhibiting of the Enola Gay certainly would not be to promote nuclear warfare, or to aggrandize nuclear warfare. The exhibit should be a factual occurrence of what happened at the end of World War II, and the airplane which was the symbol of the ending of World War II. As far as nuclear power is concerned, no official of the United States, nor leaders of its military, have ever expressed any other desire than that there should be no nuclear proliferation.

The proposed Enola Gay exhibit cannot be explained from any reasonable standpoint. The exhibit "the Final Act: The Atomic Bomb and the End of World War II" was explained by some writers as an attempt to bridge the gap between pre-atomic and atomic age youths and citizens. They suggested that this was a typical split between those of the World War II generation and those 40 and 50 years later. There should be no split between those of our age during World War II, those of the Korean War era, those of Vietnam Era, those 50 years later and those 1000 years later. That is, if history had been recorded properly and if the maudlin bleeding hearts had not taken over the writing of history and the repeating over and over that the Bomb was questionable, and repeating over and over that it was not necessary, and repeating over and over that it was barbaric. None of these are true. It should not be controversial, it should not ever be referred to as barbaric, should never be referred to as questionable. It was a correct, great, right, military, (humanitarian, if you will) decision for which future American generations should never have to apologize or defend.

Of course, it is a shame that the Enola Gay exhibits beginning with true unquestioned facts, were not exhibited. The Enola Gay, in all its glory, should have been in the original exhibit, without the distortions that Harwit and his minimally bright team had portrayed. One item historically and factually correct, was the signed receipt for the bomb materials that "the above materials were carried by Tibbets and Company to Hirohito as part of "doomsday".

The controversy over the exhibit spot-lights a glaring defect in the Smithsonian Institution; particularly the National Air and Space Museum. I question how we could put three self-proclaimed 'know-it-alls' in a position to mold the minds of future generations concerning American History in such a distorted way. How can we explain such weird people being placed in positions of authority such as Directors of the National Air and Space Museum?

This clan of "intelligentsia", while apparently trying to give their enlightened modern 'spin' to the anti-nuclear agenda would have (only if they had not been stopped) succeeded in the deracination of the very soul of our greatest triumph. That Harwit and his ilk were almost able to take upon themselves the real distorted molding of the history of the end of World War II in the most visited Museum on earth, is frightening.

During the controversy over the proposed Enola Gay exhibit, two authors who were writing a book critical of the dropping of the Atom Bomb wrote to the New York Times "it has never been easy to reconcile dropping the bomb with ourselves as decent people." They blame the lack of an impartial examination of the bomb on "misleading official explanations and government secrecy". This is trash, as far as journalism is concerned because the American people, or the government, have never made any misleading statements about the use of the Atomic Bomb, and there has been no government secrecy about the bomb. These two authors, Robert Jay Lifton and Greg Mitchell are writing this without any real thought or expertise; falling in line with the Japanese propaganda to make us feel guilty about ending the war.

We are not guilty.

We do not feel guilty.

We don't want anyone to tell us that we should feel guilty.

We don't want anyone to reflect on our decency for dropping the bomb.

We **thinking** Americans have a Clear Conscience about the Bomb. This revisionism is some 'crazy political correctness' that has come about by distorted thinking, derived from 50 years of Japanese propaganda, in trying to divert any attention from the most horrible atrocities known to mankind, by the Japanese, prior to and during World War II.

Deborah Sanders, a columnist for the San Francisco Chronicle, said that: "good history was a casualty" at the proposed Smithsonian Enola Gay exhibit. Actually she should have said that good history has been a casualty ever since the Atomic Bomb was dropped, because of the incessant propaganda of the Japanese leaders and because of the weird repeating of this by Political Correctionists who know nothing of what they are saying.

Political Correctionists, as a matter of fact, should praise the bomb because it created peace rapidly. It is a historical and national disgrace that the Enola Gay is not enshrined, totally, at the Smithsonian as a symbol of a totally correct military option.

We all hope that the dropping of the bomb will be a deterrent to any one starting a nuclear war; and it has been to this point. As a matter of fact, the number of wild liberal sycophants and Political Correctionists who are parroting the Japanese 50 year propaganda have little logic in their quirky preaching against the Atomic Bomb.

A respected writer, Dr. Thomas Sowell of the Hoover Institution has very aptly pointed out that the revisionist line:

"we didn't need to bomb because in an invasion we would have only

20,000 casualties and Japan would have been defeated in 90 days"

would be funny if it were not so sick. He wrote that leaders who knew, including British Prime Minister Winston Churchill expected a million American casualties and a half-million British casualties. Dr. Thomas Sowell is a Senior Fellow with the Hoover Institution at Stanford University, Palo Alto, California and served in the U.S. Marine Corps.

The Atomic Bomb has neither started nor participated in any war since its sole use in ending World War II.

It is to be noted that through the efforts of Brig. General Paul W. Tibbets, the Air Force Association, Veterans of Foreign Wars, American Legion, right-thinking members of Congress, and others; the Enola Gay Exhibit was finally placed in the National Air and Space Museum in a "more reasonably correct" historical display. This was done over the howls of the weirdos like Robert Jay Lifton, Greg Mitchell, Tom Crouch, Ph.D. (Project Manager, Original Exhibit) Michael J. Neufeld, Ph.D. (Curator, Original Exhibit), Gar Alperovitz and a few others.

CHAPTER 7

Truman's Decision

The first of August, 1945, President Harry Truman knew that he was mandated to order the dropping of the Atomic Bomb on Japan. There was an invasion plan, OPERATION DOWNFALL (First Phase being Operation Olympic, the Invasion of Kyushu Island), which was scheduled for November 1, 1945 to begin the invasion of the main Japanese islands (the Second Phase being Operation Coronet, the invasion of Honshu Island, to begin March 1, 1946). The invasion at its height would involve some 5,000,000 Allied military personnel, most being those of the United States of America.

President Truman knew that defending against any invasion were 2,300,000 Japanese regular troops, supplemented by another 4,000,000 Army and Navy personnel in a militia type organization, 25,000,000 people in addition (women, men and children) were mustered to supplement all of these defenders.

Note: In the 3 month period of Aug., Sept. and Oct. leading up to Nov. 1, 1945, the invasion date, this number of regular Japanese troops would increase dramatically as many of thousands were being brought back from China and Southeast Asia to defend the homeland. The number of regular troops could be expected to reach 3,000,000 by Nov. 1, 1945.

President Harry Truman

Japanese women were trained to "fight to the death" when an invasion came.

He knew that they were pledged to "fight to the death" in defense of the Emperor and the homeland. He also knew of the history of the previous 4 years in which the American and Allied forces had reached this point in the Pacific War. The President had to analyze previous battles with the Japanese and how those battles had ended in casualties. Beginning with the bloody battle of Guadalcanal in which so many American lives were taken and in which there was never any surrender by the Japanese, and then one by one analyzing the different island campaigns to see exactly what occurred by numbers.

One only needs to spotlight about 5 of the last campaigns in the Pacific to realize what President Harry Truman knew would be the results of an invasion of Japan. In naming some 5 campaigns these authors do not mean to detract from, or belittle, the importance of, nor the savage defense of, any particular territory by the Japanese, nor the heroic efforts of the United States and Allied troops in stepping stone across the Pacific Isles (Guadalcanal, Tarawa etc.) to get to the place where the Allies found themselves on August 1, 1945. Likewise, great heroic efforts in the Southeast Asia, China and Indonesian theaters and all other areas can not be forgotten. These listed campaigns will show that casualties would be tremendous in the invasion of Japan.

Mariana Islands

The Mariana Campaign began with the invasion of Saipan, June 15, 1944 with the island being secured July 9, 1944. Tinian nearby was secured August 1, 1944 and the island of Guam was invaded July 21, 1944 and secured by the Americans on August 10, 1944. On Saipan alone, the United States incurred some 17,752 casualties. The Japanese incurred some 25,000 to 30,000 deaths of which 4,300 Japanese died in suicide charges against United States troops after Saipan was, in effect, secured. Their commander, Japanese Lieutenant General Yoshitsugu Saito committed suicide after telling his troops to follow him 'he was going to seek out the enemy'.

Even after the suicide charge against our troops, in which the 4,300 Japanese died, many Japanese leaped off the cliffs from the northern end of Saipan in senseless suicide (or do the Japanese claim these were meaningful?).

An interesting note for movie-goers; Lee Marvin of Hollywood fame, "Dirty Dozen", "Paint Your Wagon", "The Man Who Shot Liberty Valance", "Cat Ballou" and many other, was in the U.S. Marine Corps, having been on a number of invasions prior to Saipan, and on Saipan, of 247 Marines in I Company, 4th Marine Regiment, 4th Marine Division, only he and 5 others survived. He was wounded and evacuated on the hospital ship "Solace" and spent 13 months hospitalized. The "Solace" was later the victim, along with its nurses and medical personnel, of a Kamikaze attack (described later in this book), by one of the Emperor's "heroes."

On Tinian almost all of the Japanese were killed because of their resistance and determination to die for the Emperor. The United States had some 1800 casualties on Tinian. On Guam the United States casualties were approximately 7,000 and there were very few Japanese who surrendered on Guam, although because of the dense jungle on Guam many Japanese went into the hills and jungles of Guam and survived for a long period of time. Many did not ever surrender even after the surrender of the high command in Japan. [That will be touched on in another chapter]

Peleliu Island

The next brutal campaign after Guam was the battle of Peleliu. This battle began on September 15, 1944 and the island was declared secured on October 12, 1944. In this battle it was predicted that it would require only one month to complete and while the island may have been declared secure on October 12, 1944 there were not only deadly skirmishes which continued for quite some time but, as will be pointed out later, some of the Japanese stayed in caves for a long time after the island had been declared secure and quite a lengthy time after the Japanese high command had surrendered in Japan, and the war was over.

This brutal campaign cost the United States 8,387 casualties and of the 10,695 Japanese originally on the island all were killed except 301 who were captured. The tenacity of the Japanese on

Peleliu was, as in all of these islands, unrelenting and they were determined to kill as many United States personnel as possible knowing that they would be killed if they did not surrender, and they had no idea of surrendering.

Again, faced with the absolute knowledge that they would be annihilated the entire Japanese garrison fought to the end with no hope of winning this battle.

Listen to a man I consider the "Ultimate Marine", who fought on Peleliu and gives us for this book, an insight into what the Japanese home island invasion would be like.

"On Peleliu Island we encountered the first of those Japanese home-land types of defense in depth where the defenders were ordered to fight until killed in their positions.

The Japanese had been on Peleliu since seizing it from the Germans after World War I. Under the high ridges were five levels of caves. Cannons from sunken ships were in the mouths of caves with steel doors which opened when they were ready to fire. Machine guns forty feet back in caves fired bursts out of small apertures.

Their efforts at fortification were concealed by heavy jungle foliage and by removing local natives from the island.

Our limited efforts at reconnaissance failed to detect the defenses, leading our senior commanders to announce a "cake walk", "all over in two days." We were in the middle of these heavy defenses soon after landing. Our Division lost 6000 casualties in the first four days. Each Japanese defender "killed Americans until he, himself, was killed."

— General Ray Davis

In line with the comments of General Davis concerning the "Cake Walk" it should be noted that the bombardment of Peleliu had ceased before the Marine landing, as the battleships and cruisers had proclaimed that there were "no more significant targets to be shelled." The Marines found the hidden defenses to be almost without damage when they went on Peleliu.

General Raymond Davis, U.S. Marine Corps (Retired), received the Navy Cross, Purple Heart and other medals for his part in Peleliu. He also fought on Guadalcanal, Korea where he received the Medal of Honor for the Chosin Reservoir battle and Vietnam. He was later appointed Assistant Commandant of the U. S. Marine Corps.

Iwo Jima Island

The next campaign was the brutal one for Iwo Jima. It began February 19, 1945 and the island was declared secured March 26, 1945. Statistically this was the worst for the United States of any of the battles. It involved some 71,245 Marines ready to take the island. 10,087 Marines, Navy personnel, Navy doctors, Corpsmen and other personnel (3,266) were killed with a total of 26,038 casualties on Iwo Jima. Of the 23,000 Japanese on the island all except 216 were killed. These being the only ones taken prisoner. It was not the aim of the Japanese to ever be taken prisoner, but to die for the Emperor and the homeland, and to kill as many as possible for the Emperor.

A very significant part of the Iwo Jima battle was the fact that for some 2 1/2 months before the Marines invaded Iwo Jima the island was under constant air and naval bombardment. Naval bombardment from battleships, their 16 inch guns and cruiser bombardment, and from air bombardment is a disastrous occurrence on an island of this size; some 5 miles long. Yet with all of this bombardment the Japanese had a complete garrison holed up in bunkers, caves and tunnels to oppose the Marines at the time of their landing.

The terrible statistics of Iwo Jima would certainly illustrate what would occur on any invasion of Japan as their mindset was to kill as many Americans as possible before they all were certainly to be killed.

The Philippines

This campaign began in the last part of 1944 and, being such a huge group of large islands, it continued until July of 1945. The United States incurred some 80,000 casualties in the Philippine campaign.

While the Philippine campaign was no less vicious on the part of the Japanese in fighting to the death; one of the more significant and horrifying features of this campaign was that, as the Japanese were being defeated and their capture or withdrawal in the Philippines, and particularly in Manila, was eminent, they slaughtered 100,000 Filipinos as a barbaric final act in the Philippines.

This gives a vivid illustration as to what the Japanese homeland islands would be like for all of those prisoners there and elsewhere in the Japanese prisoner of war camps. At Leyte the Japanese sacrificed their entire garrison of over 50,000. The magnitude of their losses here was huge.

Another little gruesome occurrence was brought to light when survivors in the Philippines stated that on December 14, 1944, Japanese guards herded 150 Americans into bunkers used for air raid shelters, threw gasoline and blazing torches on them and when the screaming victims tried to escape they were bayoneted or machine-gunned. This is a true account by some survivors.

The Philippine campaign saw the first use of the Kamikaze, or suicide airplane, by the Japanese. A pilot wishing to sacrifice his life for the Emperor would dive his airplane into a ship or military installation seeking only to kill as many Americans as he could as he plunged to his death. Recruited Kamikaze pilots, unwilling to die for the Emperor in a suicide attack, were disgraced and imprisoned, and executed.

Okinawa

Okinawa involved an island south of the mainland of Japan and this campaign was on an island some 60 miles long and 2 to 18 miles wide. Some 550,000 United States military personnel were involved in the operation and it resulted in 68,000 casualties to the United States. For the Japanese practically all of their defense forces, 80,000 regular troops and 20,000 of the home defense were killed leaving only a very few captured. A startling figure from this campaign was that 150,000 civilians were killed during this operation. A great number of these civilian casualties were not from bombardment or from casual gunfire on both sides, but a great number of these civilians were used mercilessly by the Japanese, sending them toward the American lines at night to draw fire, and also sending them to explode hidden mines.

Again the Japanese fought with only one thing in mind, to kill as many as possible before they were defeated; and they knew that their defeat, and death, was inevitable.

The invasion of Okinawa involved 4 Army and 2 Marine divisions. It was comparable to the Normandy landing with the original assault totaling 150,000 men. There was a 1,300 ship fleet in the operation. Army and Marine forces had 68,000 casualties.

The Okinawa battle also demonstrated in a more far reaching and deadly manner how the Japanese would use the kamikaze (suicide) planes. The air attacks exceeded anything previously encountered from the Japanese (being so close to Japan; only 350 miles). The Japanese committed 6,000 plus aircraft to the battle; of which 3,000 were kamikazes. 35 United States Navy ships were sunk and 350 ships were damaged, **with the United States Navy suffering more casualties than the combined total of all its previous wars.**

Lessons Learned

These five campaigns taught us the following five things:

1. **The Japanese would not surrender just by being overwhelmed in battle.** They had no chance of winning, or even of survival on Iwo Jima, Peleliu, Saipan or Tinian. Many would hide in the jungles of Guam or the Philippines, but none surrendered because of the imminent defeat.

2. **As General Ray Davis described; we saw what their "homeland types of defense" would be.** We knew with the resources and personnel in the main Japanese islands being devoted to building bunkers, pill-boxes, endless tunnels and traps and their resolve to stay in these hidden caves and defenses to their death, that casualties would far exceed those horrible ones previously experienced. According to General Davis and others; when viewed after the Japanese surrender, the intricate death traps and defenses on Kyushu, Shikoku and Honshu were even

more deadly than they had imagined.

> *"In predicting casualties for the invasion of Japan, my experience on Peleliu and my knowledge of the great number of divisions of U.S. military personnel, (including all six (6) divisions of the U.S. Marine Corps) together with my observation (post-war) of the awesome defenses on Kyushu and Honshu, which would be encountered in the invasion, leads me to believe that any casualty estimates would have to range in the 1 million to 2 million range.*

> — General Ray Davis

Being in the initial Olympic Operations assault force and in the initial Coronet Operation assault force it has been reasonably predicted (and I sadly agree) that the Marine Corps Force would have ceased to exist, after the invasion.

3. **The Kamikaze aircraft the Japanese had in reserve would inflict frightful damage from ship to shore (up to 16,000 of these).**

4. **Civilian deaths could be in the range of 20 million.** There would be no slaughter of civilians by the Japanese, as in the Philippines, but the 150,000 civilian deaths on Okinawa told much about what deaths would be on the main Japanese islands, with some 75,000,000 inhabitants at the time.

5. **Allied casualties would be numbered in millions using any reasonable analysis of the Okinawa and the other campaigns.**

CHAPTER 8

Wait for Surrender – An Alternative to the Bomb

There is no reasonable basis for believing the theory of the Revisionists that the Japanese were ready to surrender or even would surrender. Lifton and Mitchell, in their book, *Hiroshima in America*, assert that the Japanese would probably have surrendered by November 1, 1945 and most definitely by December 31, 1945.

While they give absolutely no factual basis for these assertions, let's assume (without admitting) that they might be correct. Would the casualties stand still until those dates arrive? No.

Massive daily B-29 raids would occur. Naval bombardments and carrier aircraft raids would be constant. The 16,000 or so Kamikaze aircraft of the Japanese would exact a tremendous toll in ships and lives on our fleet, as would the suicide submarines, suicide boats and suicide manned torpedoes, and suicide human mines.

From August 6, 1945 through December 31, 1945 one can easily predict hundreds of thousands of casualties. You also (with the invasion being imminent) can write off all the Allied prisoners, detainees and prisoners of all the occupied countries. The Japanese High Command Order to slaughter all of these would assuredly be enforced.

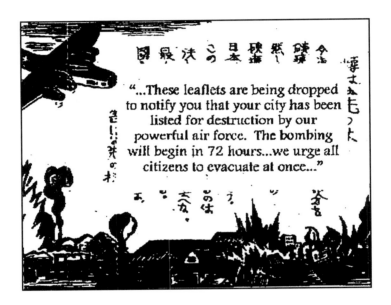

Although Japan gave no warning prior to bombing Pearl Harbor, the U.S. Air Force dropped hundreds of thousands of the leaflets (as shown here) prior to bombing Japanese cities in 1945. Revisionist historians never give credit for this historic, humanitarian gesture.

Kill them all order Jan. 8, 1944

The original Japanese order to execute prisoners of war if Japan was invaded — 1945, to "kill them all" and "leave no traces". The original is now in the U.S. National Archives in Washington, DC.

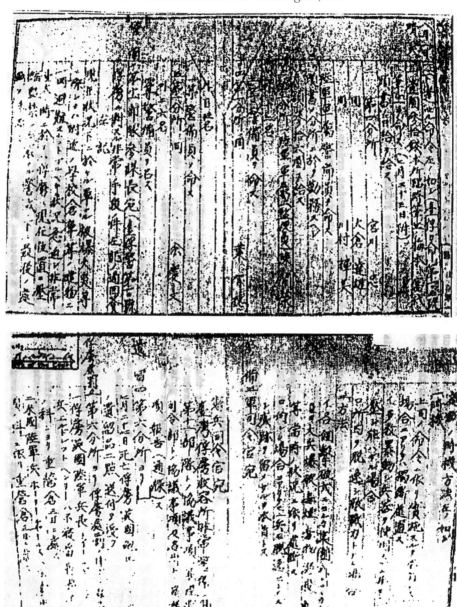

CLEAR CONSCIENCE – The Atom Bomb vs. The Super Holocaust

KILL THEM ALL ORDER
1/8/1944

Document No. 2701

(Certified as Exhibit "O" in D.c. No. 2687)

From the Journal of the Taiwan POW Camp H.Q. in Taihoku

Entry 1st August, 1944

(entries about money, promotions of Formosans at Branch camps, including promotion of Yo Yu-toku 1st Cl Keibiin — 5 entries).

The following answer about the extreme measures for POWs was sent to the Chief of Staff of the 11th Unit (Formosa POW Security No. 10).

"Under the present situation if there were a mere explosion or fire a shelter for the time being could be had in nearby buildings such as the school, a warehouse, or the like. However, at such time as the situation became urgent and it be extremely important, the POWs will be concentrated and confined in their present location and under heavy guard the preparation for the final disposition will be made.

The time and method of this disposition are as follows:

(1) The Time.

Although the basic aim is to act under superior orders, individual disposition may be made in the following circumstances:

    (a) When an uprising of large numbers cannot be suppressed without the use of firearms.

    (b) When escapes from the camp may turn into a hostile fighting force.

(2) The Methods.

    (a) Whether they are destroyed individually or in groups, or however it is done, with mass bombing, poisonous smoke, poisons, drowning, decapitation, or what, dispose of them as the situation dictates.

    (b) In any case it is the aim not to allow the escape of a single one, to annihilate them all, and not to leave any traces.

(3) To: The Commanding General

    The Commanding General of Military Police
    Reported matters conferred on with the 11th Unit,
    the Keelung Fortified Are H.Q., and each
    prefecture concerning the extreme security in
    Taiwan POW Camps."

Document No. 2687
(Certified as Exhibit "J" in Doc. No. 2687)

To: Chief of Staff, Taiwan Army
From: Chief Prisoner of War Camps Tokyo
          POW Camps Radio 80 Top Military Secret.
          20 August 1945

     Personnel who mistreated prisoners of war and internees or who are held in extremely bad sentiment by them are permitted to take care of it by immediately transferring or by fleeing without trace. Moreover, documents which would be unfavorable for us in the hands of the enemy are to be treated in the same way as secret documents and destroyed when finished with.

Addressees: Korean Army, Taiwan Army, Xwantung (Manchuria) Army, North China Area Army, Hong Kong.
               Chiefs of Staff — Korea, Taiwan, Mukden, Borneo, North China, Hong Kong, Thailand, Malaya, Java.
               PW Camp Commanding Officer.

     I hereby certify that this is a true translation from Taiwan Army H.Q. Staff files concerning POWs. Vol. 7.

                       Signed: Stephen H. Green
                                STEPHEN H. GREEN

     This is Exhibit marked "J", referred to in the Affidavit of JAMES THOMAS NEHEMIAH CROSS.

     Sworn before me this 19th day of September, 1948.
                    / s /   P. A. L. Vine
                             Major E. N.

For most people, considering all other circumstances, the key as to whether or not to drop the Atomic Bombs, was whether or not the Japanese were, in August 1945, ready to surrender. If they were ready to surrender, the bombs should not be dropped. If they were not ready to surrender, the bombs should be dropped.

Now this thinking is not the reasoning of the few wild correctionists mentioned in this book, such as Robert J. Lifton, Greg Mitchell, Gar Alpervitz, Professor Neufeld, Dr. Harwit or Dr. Crouch. They would have preferrerd, even though the Japanese would not surrender at all, to risk our millions of servicemen in an invasion of Japan rather than drop the Atomic Bomb. You will recall Professor Neufeld stating that "the casualties anticipated in an invasion were irrelevant to President Truman's decision to drop the bomb." Of course, this statement ranks with, and might exceed, any of the more stupid historical statements ever made.

In any event, let's examine the evidence concerning whether or not the Japanese were ready to surrender.

1. The only real evidence that the Japanese should surrender was the condition of their military forces, their depletion of their air naval power, their major cities being in ruins, their war production capacity being greatly depleted.

2. The only other circumstantial evidence that they were ready to surrender was that after the surrender, a few (very few) of the Japanese leaders said, "Oh! We were ready to surrender, they should not have dropped the Atomic Bomb." (Now let's give a lot of credence to this belated self-serving declaration.)

On the other side of the circumstantial evidence concerning a surrender would be these factors:

1. They proclaimed loud and long that they would never surrender.

2. They had prepared unbelievable defenses in the Japanese islands including withdrawing most of their armies from outside Japan to defend the homelands and had mobilized the entire population of Japan for this purpose.

3. Their leaders were feverishly negotiating with the Russians to allow them to join with the Japanese in a coalition to get them to divide up Eastern Asia and China. The Japanese to be the Naval power, and between the two of them would have the largest army in the world.

4. Their national war slogan was at this times, "One Hundred Million Die Together" (all of this for the Sun God Emperor). It should be noted that there were probably 75,000,000 Japanese in the homeland at that time and they were including in their "hundred million" all of the Japanese outside of the home islands to be sacrificed in this last glorious bang.

5. The most positive evidence that the Japanese were not ready to surrender is included in the last battles listed in this book. Saipan: they should have surrendered in Saipan, they were going to be defeated, they were going to die, but instead of any surrender in Saipan, they inflicted 17,000 casualties against the Americans and sacrificed 30,000 Japanese including 4,500 suicides.

    They should have surrendered on Tinian, they were going to be killed; they should have surrendered on Guam, they should have surrendered on Peleliu, such a small island with no hope of escape and only fighting to kill Americans and die for the Emperor.

Then Iwo Jima; here is an island with 23,000 Japanese, totally isolated, surrounded by enemy ships and invasion forces and no hope of winning at all and no surrender.

The same could be said of all of the for Okinawa, and in addition to their glorious fighting to the death they took 150,000 civilians; men, women, children, babies with them (don't talk to me about the men, women and children of Hiroshima).

Some historians believe the threat to life was more extensive. John L. Glen, Historian for the Sugano Prison Association and former member of the military garrison which held Japanese war criminals after the war, claims there were almost 800,000 captives in Southern Asia alone.

If there needed to be any more circumstantial evidence that the Japanese High Command was not ready to surrender before August 6th it so happened that even after the second Atomic Bomb was dropped half of the Japanese High Command was not in favor of surrender.

There was great turmoil within the Japanese High Command and there was almost a civil insurrection at the highest level, with the killing of some who were proposing surrender and finally there were the hardliners who were opposed to any surrender as long as they had the huge military armies available to them. Many of these hardliners had to be killed or overcome before the ones in favor of surrender, and the Emperor, could proclaim that the Japanese were going to surrender.

These historically correct professors such as Lifton etc., obviously do not understand circumstantial evidence.

The Mike Tyson/Evander Holyfield ear biting incident reminded me of an illustration which we had in court many years before, concerning circumstancial evidence. The case was a prosecution for "maiming another" and the principal witness had stated that the defendent bit off the ear of the injured party. The witness had stated that the defendent bit off the other man's ear. He had repeated this and then had observed that he was not looking right at the defendent when the ear was bitten off. Seizing upon this, in a positive way, the defense counsel asked, "You did not see him bite the ear off?"

"No" said the witness.

The lawyer asked, "You actually were not looking at him at the time you say the defendent bit the ear off?"

"No," said the witness.

"And yet you tell us that you know positively that the defendent bit off the man's ear?" asked the lawyer.

"Yes," said the witness.

Then the lawyer asked, "How do you know positively that he bit the man's ear off if you did not see him bite it?"

"I saw him spit it out." answered the witness.

Case Closed.

The Japanese did not surrender after the first bomb was dropped. No other evidence needs to supplement the rest of the evidence that they were not ready to surrender.

They were not ready to surrender.

CHAPTER 9

The Final Facts

The Kamikazes would be a huge factor in the invasion of Japan as there were as many as 16,000 kamikaze airplanes in waiting on the main islands of Japan, and there were hundreds of small suicide midget submarines, suicide boats and human torpedoes waiting to attack the Naval Armada used in the invasion. Kamikazes had been used almost entirely against naval vessels during the Okinawa campaign, but during the Japan invasion they, along with other suicide apparatus, would have been used on troop concentrations to inflict maximum casualties on landing troops. The beach-head assault troops would have tremendous casualties, above anything previously experienced.

President Truman's concern was, of course, primarily the number of casualties of the Allies. Incidentally, the number of deaths which would occur to the Japanese, should also be considered. Any reasonable analysis of the figures concerning Allied casualties in an invasion of Japan dictates that there would, in all probability be upwards of 1,000,000 deaths and upwards of 2,000,000 casualties in the invasion. The estimate of the initial 1,000,000 man D-Day invasion force (Operation Olympic) indicated 30 to 35 percent casualties within the **first 30 days**. 350,000 casualties within 30 days is tremendous. The initial fact to be considered was that the Japanese had totally, irrevocably, rejected surrender, as laid out by the Potsdam Declaration.

One of the greatest, if not the greatest, considerations of the military and President Truman were the 150,000 United States and Allied prisoners. In addition, there were Chinese, Korean, Southeast Asian, and military and civilian prisoners and detainees of other countries (probably approaching another 300,00), in the hands of the Japanese. Making some 450,000 people subject to slaughter under the Japanese Imperial command order to dispose of them in any manner upon the approach of an invasion of the home islands of Japan.

In addition to the 150,000 Allied prisoners of war, who would be eliminated entirely in the event of an invasion, think of what would happen to the people who were subjugated, and under the military power of Japan with absolutely no defense at all. As the invasion of Japan became a reality one can predict quite easily (based on the recent Philippine massacres) what would have occurred with occupied and unliberated countries and islands, as the Japanese could see that area being liberated, and one can certainly imagine how many more Chinese would have also been killed and the country exploited by the Japanese military force whose homeland had been defeated entirely. The numbers of Chinese, Koreans, Southeast Asians and others being killed would be staggering. As a matter of fact, the numbers slaughtered **after** the surrender of Japan were staggering.

It was stated by the President and the Joint Chief's of Staff, leading up to the use of the bomb, that the invasion would create another Okinawa from one end of Japan to the other.

Faced with casualties approximating 1,500,000 or more of United States and Allied forces and 2,000,000 or more of the Japanese military forces and using the Okinawa campaign as a guideline it could be estimated that some 20,000,000 or more civilians could be killed in the giant operation of invading the Japanese islands, Truman decided to end the war by dropping the bomb on what were two strategic military towns. The towns of Hiroshima and Nagasaki were productive of military and war materials with many production facilities in both cities and were, of course, legitimate targets.

A tremendous salient point concerning the Atom Bomb and the claim of lack of compassion by Americans, is that beginning in July, Americans dropped leaflets telling which cities would be bombed, so that the civilians could be forewarned and evacuate. (This by airmen who were being beheaded at anytime their plane was downed over Japan).

Quite relevant in the selection of Atom Bomb targets was that five cities on Honshu had not received major damage; Kyoto (which was to be spared because of being the cultural and historic center) Niigata, Kokura, Hiroshima and Nagasaki.

The magic decrypts, of intercepted messages from the Japanese headquarters, proclaimed the following about the upcoming invasion:

1. All prisoners were to be killed (150,000 U.S. and Allied prisoners, with a possible count of military and political prisoners and detainees of other countries swelling this to 450,000 at risk under this order.)

2. All of the armed and related forces of the country were to fight to the death.

3. They were to take as many enemy lives as possible while they were dying.

4. The Japanese Generals totally rejected the Potsdam Declaration, and its surrender terms, and the Decrypts showed that the Japanese were never serious in negotiating a surrender.

5. They were trying to make a deal with the Russians to get the Russians to pursue the non-aggression pact between the two nations and divide China, and all Eastern and Southeastern Asia between the two powers, Russia and Japan.

As late as July 3, 1945, Koki Hirota, a Japanese diplomat, with Emperor Hirohito's blessing, was working for a deal with the Russians whereby Japan would increase its naval strength and in joining with the Russian army, would have a force unequaled in the world. This would leave Japan in almost its same military stance as it had at the beginning of the war with the United States and the bombing of Pearl Harbor. Dominating a large portion of China,

Southeast Asia and the Western Pacific.

The Magic Summaries, or intercepts, also revealed that all through June and July of 1945 Japan's military leaders had adamantly determined that they would never surrender unconditionally to the Americans.

The Japanese High Command, the Military Leaders and the Emperor killed those people at Hiroshima and Nagasaki; not the Atomic Bomb, not President Truman, and not the United States of America.

The Japanese whining about the Bomb calls to mind a young man who murdered both parents and his plea in court was for sympathy and mercy, because he was an orphan.

Instead of asking questions about the use of the Atomic Bomb by President Truman; Americans should be answering all of the questions. They should not let the terrible atrocious acts of the Japanese military be forgotten through a distortion of history, that distortion of history being accomplished by spotlighting the Bomb.

All this about the Bomb can be compared to 50,000,000 useless deaths occurring in a Useless World War; and millions of atrocious deaths caused by a Japanese military force, never in all of history equaled in its inhuman excesses. The saga of the Japanese military past should be spot-lighted over and over and remembered, so that its excesses will never occur again.

CHAPTER 10

Deliberate Planned Distortion of History

Immediately after the signing of the surrender documents by the Japanese on September 2, 1945, the foreign minister, Mamoru Shigemitsu began a world wide propaganda campaign to brand the Americans as war criminals for using nuclear weapons. The goal of the propaganda was to keep Emperor Hirohito from being declared a War Criminal, and to divert western attention away from Japanese military atrocities committed during their China occupation prior to and during World War II, and their continued unthinkable atrocities against Allied prisoners. It was to divert world attention from their Super Holocaust (which exceeded the Nazi HOLOCAUST) everywhere in Asia and the Pacific for decades prior to and during World War II.

An intercept of Japanese Military Headquarters Communications showed that on September 15, 1945, Shigemitsu stated that since the Americans had been raising an uproar about the question of our mistreatment of prisoners, the Japanese should make every effort to exploit the Atomic Bomb question in their propaganda.

From that day until now the distortion of history has continued, and the Japanese have been able to totally spotlight the Atomic Bomb's use, as compared to Japan's Super Holocaust with its savage atrocities and killing of Chinese, other Asians and Filipinos; and their horrible treatment, bayoneting and killing of our Americans on the Bataan Death March, and the bombing of Pearl Harbor, killing thousands of our Servicemen and civilians. Our grotty group at the National Air and Space Museum and Lifton, Mitchell and Alperovitz and a few other wimps are giving them support in that distortion.

CHAPTER 11

Japanese Leadership: Suppressing the Truth

As history now stands, the world will always know the destructive power of the Atomic Bomb. We have never done anything to distort or diminish what occurred with the dropping of the bombs on Hiroshima and Nagasaki. However, unless we make sure at this point in time, that the world understands the use of the Atomic Bomb, **and its absolute correctness**, history will depict us as scoundrels.

Japanese writing and propaganda about the China War, Asian domination, Asian atrocities and World War II, and the Atomic Bomb, show that history is determined by the writer. It brings to mind a story about Winston Churchill. Upon disagreeing with a statement made by Prime Minister Stanley Baldwin, Winston

Churchill declared emphatically, "History will say that the Right Honorable Gentlemen was wrong in this matter". After a brief pause he added, "I know it will, because I shall write the history."

The Japanese are saying what this history is, because so far; **they** have been writing it.

Every August 6 and August 9, we permit the Japanese leadership to focus the entire world's attention to the pitiful scenes at Hiroshima and Nagasaki. We are made to listen to the lamentations of those suffering survivors and bereaved families who have endured through prayer. We are made to watch the symbolic, sympathetic visit of Emperor Akihito to the monuments which have been erected to honor their dead. And then, like an actor on cue, Emperor Akihito delivers his lines to a world audience and speaks of his hope "that the world deepens its understanding of nuclear weapons". He claims to pray "for the repose of the victims and peace so that humanity will never experience such a disaster again." He speaks as if he is endowed with some logia-like omniscience.

The fact remain, the suffering at Hiroshima and Nagasaki was **minuscule** compared to the over all suffering caused by the Japanese military in China, Southeast Asia, Indonesia, The Philippines, Pacific Islands, Taihoku Prison and similar Prison Camps of the Japanese, the Bataan Death March, Bombing of Pearl Harbor, Hospitals in Singapore and also the potential 20,000,000 military and civilian deaths in an invasion of Japan. Compared to this visit to Hiroshima and Nagasaki, it would be very nice if the Emperor would go to China and pray that never again will a Super-Holocaust occur wherein 30,000,000 people are killed, and where a people are used like rats as experiments to prepare the military of Japan to be able to dominate the world; or at least to dominate all of China, Southeast Asia and the entire Pacific area; and it would be nice not to continue to try to place a guilt complex on the United States of America for ending the war properly. It would also help future generations for the Japanese leadership to acknowledge specifically and not in only "pitiful generalized terms" their colonialism[4] and their atrocities.

Japanese leadership should specifically acknowledge (and document for posterity) the horrendous killings, and concentration camps all over China and Southeast Asia, document the activities of Unit 731, and the experiments on humans with anthrax, germs, plague and other biological weapons for military use. They should specifically acknowledge their "Rape of Nanking" and then we would really have something to tell the world that we hope never occurs again.

The United States of America joins with all who hope that the world will never have to experience the use of an Atomic Bomb again; nor experience a Pearl Harbor; nor a Bataan Death March; nor the killing of 40% of prisoners of war and people in concentration camps; nor the enslaving of millions of people of China and so many other small helpless countries; nor the dissecting of humans while they are alive; nor the injecting of humans with plague and other killing germs to see how long it would take them to die. We hope that there will never be another military unit like the Japanese Military Unit 731 designed to use deadly experiments on humans as if they were vermin. We hope all of these things never occur again.

Emperor Akihito would do well to allow publications by the very

---

[4] They had no real colonialism, only bloody conquering enslavement.

---

few historians in Japan who are brave enough to want to give an accurate account of the Chinese invasion by Japanese military forces, and the aggressions and horrendous, indescribable cruelty which occurred in China and through out Southeast Asia, and in the Pacific Islands. The Emperor and Japanese leaders would do well to allow these historians and the history books of the Japanese to reflect the true history prior to Pearl Harbor, and not to pass off Pearl Harbor as simply an occurrence which might, or might not, have happened. He should let Japanese history reflect that Pearl Harbor was the fault of the Japanese.

Again, I have never seen any official from Japan acknowledge that bombing our fleet in a sneak attack at Pearl Harbor, sinking a great portion of our Navy and killing thousands of Americans, was wrong.

The Emperor would do well to read Shelton H. Harris, a California State University Historian, who wrote a book on Japanese Military Unit 731, *Factories of Death*. In it, it was estimated that 200,000 Chinese were killed in germ warfare field experiments alone. The Emperor would also do well to let the Japanese history Professor Saburo Ienaga publish his books on Japan's war crimes. He has been stymied and ostracized because of his attempt to tell the truth about the Japanese atrocities and particularly Unit 731 the infamous unit conducting germ and biological experiments on thousand of humans in China. This professor's historical accounts have been censored and rejected by the education department in Japan and he has been unable to publish anything. He has taken many years to try to publish his painful and true historic accounts.

No one has ever heard anything other than a vague, non-specific mumble that the Japanese regretted the war in the Pacific. No one has ever heard any statement that the atrocities in the Bataan Death March were wrong.

With this unbelievable propaganda campaign begun immediately after signing surrender documents, they have been almost able to obliterate from the eyes of the world their vicious military history. We must not let this continue to happen, **at our expense**.

Immediately after the end of the war, the Japanese decided they were the World Conscience on the Bomb, and on War, and Peace. They first must have a conscience about their brutal unequaled, horrendous, military history before they start in on our conscience. As we say in the South, because the Bomb was dropped on them, it didn't "make their mouths into a prayer book."

CHAPTER 12

German Nazis vs. Japanese Imperial Army

The Japanese Military must be compared to the German Nazis. The German Nazis brutally killed 6,000,000 Jews in a vile attempt to exterminate that race of people. The Germans under Hitler, proclaimed that they were a Master Race destined to rule the world. The Germans had a secret police force, The Gestapo, which could brutalize prisoners, civilians and anyone they chose, selectively. The Nazis and Gestapo of Germany are well documented in history. **Nothing can minimize the brutality of the Nazis, particularly to the Jews.**

Japanese Prison Camp Casualties = 100%

From about 1935 forward, beginning with the teachings of Colonel Hashimoto, the Greater Japan Young Men's Society taught the young men of Japan that they were a master race prepared for world domination. Just an example of routine practice for the Japanese Army was the murdering of 100 American Prisoners of War on Wake Island, October 7, 1943.

As compared to the Germans Nazis; the entire Japanese Imperial Army was a killing and torture machine, treating all other people, including babies, children and women, as vermin or rodents to be bayoneted, to be dissected alive, to be cut open alive by scalpel, to be infected with plague or any disease for experimentation, to have their eyes punched out, to have their genitals cut off, to have their limbs cut off without anesthetic and while alive, and many other brutalities which might occur to a "Knight of Bushido." The Bushido Code authorized the Japanese soldier to do anything cruel, sadistic or deadly in the name of the military, or the Emperor. The Japanese had the Kempei Tai, which was the Japanese Gestapo. The Kempei Tai carried out all the above described torture activity routinely on all prisoners and civilians. Kempei Tai torturing and killings dwarfed anything ever attributable to the Gestapo.

Compared to the German Nazis and the Gestapo, the Japanese Imperial Army had Unit 731. Unit 731 was the most cruel and heinous of all Japanese Units, or of all Military Units ever. Unit 731 was the medical, biological, experimental unit which operated in China and specialized in incomprehensible dissecting of live humans to see how long it would take them to die from the loss of an organ or from an injection, or from plague, and to observe the results of deadly experiments before the unfortunate victim actually died. One of Unit 731's last acts after the surrender was to release plague infected rats near Harbin, China causing more than 30,000 deaths alone.

The routine torture or killing of prisoners by Germans did not occur. Some 3% of prisoners of war died in German prison camps, compared to almost 45% of Americans killed in Japanese prisoner of war camps. In addition to the unthinkable death toll in prison camps, 100% of the prisoners were subjected to the most inhuman starvation, torture, and humiliation ever conceived. Also torture and death await-ed any who tried to escape, with the Japanese making an example of them in front of other prisoners, such as tying them to a stake and bayoneting them, or hanging them from a wire and beating them to death. Any excuse to murder a prisoner. Not that it mattered to the Japanese, but all International Treaties prohibited punishment of a prisoner of war for trying to escape.

When we speak of prison camp statistics we list the percent of those who died in death camps and when we write about battles we talk of death and injuries and **total** casualties. It needs to be pointed out that in using deaths and those wounded as "casualties" the Allies had virtually 100% casualties in Japanese prison camps. No prisoners of the Japanese survived who did not have the equivalent of battle wounds. If it wasn't through bayoneting, beating injuries or tor-ture, then it was through starvation. Yes, 100% casualties.

Would you call these P.O.W.s casualties?

CHAPTER 13

Revisionists vs. Truman and the Truth

As previously stated; during the 50 year anniversary of the dropping of the Atomic Bombs, the Mayor of Nagasaki, during a so-called peace program, said "let history decide whether the Atomic Bomb was correct".

I repeat, if we let these idiotic sayings go unanswered, and if we wait until all involved in World War II and the dropping of the bomb (and really those with the only true perspective) are gone, and let the Japanese and obscurants like Harwit and the others continue to distort World War II and the Atomic Bomb, and Japanese history, the Japanese will have determined "history" for all time.

The Japanese will have (and already have to a great extent) determined our history for us, unless we correct these distortions and lies now.

The Japanese writers and historians have not only distorted their own history for their future Japanese generations but they have solicited help from non-thinkers like Gar Alperovitz, Harwit and his group at the National Air and Space Museum, and authors Robert Lifton and Greg Mitchell to participate in their revisionist writing and they have people like this who trumpet the fact that anyone who disagrees with them is a revisionist. This reverse-revisionist psychology is similar to the Japanese trying to reverse our roles as aggressor and victim in the Pacific War by constantly hammering at the Atomic Bomb. We should never let these people write history for us.

Professor Ronald Spector, Professor of History and International Relations at George Washington University's Elliot School of International Affairs said that Gar Alperovitz had been pedaling his revisionist line for 40 years. This Revisionist line constantly proclaimed: "there is no consensus about whether the bomb ended the War sooner or not. And there is no consensus on whether the invasion of Japan would have been necessary or not. And there is no consensus on what the casualties may have been on the invasion of Japan." Winston Churchill placed the predicted casualties in an invasion of Japan at 1,200,000 with Americans being 1,000,000 of these.

The only reason that some mindless writer can assert that there is no consensus on these topics is that Alperovitz, Lifton and Mitchell and their ilk all have written long, and spoken loud, about the Bomb so as to create the impression that there is no consensus on any of the facts surrounding the use of the Atomic Bomb. The old adage: "if you repeat something long enough and loud enough, people will believe it" is too true.

Opposed to that shallow unreasonable line of thought, and as a matter of fact, among all those who have any desire to know the truth, and who knew the facts at the time President Harry Truman ordered the dropping of the Bomb, there is really unanimity and a total consensus about the valid and proper use of the Atomic Bomb.

Winston Churchill asserted about the decision to drop the bomb; "to avert a **vast indefinite butchery**, to bring the war to an end, to give peace to the world, to laying healing hands upon its tortured peoples by manifestation of overwhelming power at the cost of a few explosions, seem, after all our toils and perils, a miracle of deliverance." The statement of this great British Statesman, added to all of the other facts surrounding the bomb, should determine for all time that the use of the bomb was proper.

Actually an Interim Committee, along with Secretary of War Henry Stimson and all the chief advisors to the President, recommended use of the Bomb on a real target.

When a respected journalist, William Leonard Lawrence, assigned to the Atom Bomb project wrote most favorably about the decision to drop the bomb, he was criticized by Lifton and Mitchell for being Jewish and having an anti-Holocaust background. How is that for a little anti-Semitism?

Let me quote the final two sentences of the chapter in Lifton and Mitchell's book where they summarize how wrong President Truman's decision was:

"His decision was prefigured but not foreclosed. In the end he decided to use atomic weapons on undefended cities because he was drawn to their power and because he was afraid not to use them."

What Journalistic Licentiousness! Undefended Cities!! This was injected into the book to try to make President Truman seem heartless. Hiroshima and Nagasaki were as well defended as any Japanese city on Honshu or Kyushu. "Undefended" meant absolutely nothing in this bombing.

Probably the ultimate in idiotic sayings and the most nauseating to this writer, was in this book *Hiroshima in America* by Lifton and Mitchell where they demeaned President Harry Truman.[5]

They said: "Truman emerges as neither hero nor villain, and certainly not as the model of control and country wisdom (enshrined in the misleading saying "The buck stops here!") but as a tragic figure unable or unwilling to recognize, to touch emotionally, either his own tragedy or the human tragedy of the atomic bombings." They acknowledged that President Truman brought "statesmanlike" insight, energy and courage to every crisis" and was clear-sighted "within his horizons." Going on to say his "horizons" were not broad enough to provide the extraordinary wisdom demanded by the atomic age. In the next breath, they questioned whether anyone would have "mustered greater wisdom." (The implication here is that only these two authors, by hindsight, have that greater wisdom.)

This, along with the rest of their pompous prolixity, was garbage. How disgraceful! How sickening! To attempt to degrade one of the most momentous proper decision-makers in all of history. For the information of these two literary geniuses, Harry Truman had a Masters Degree in Human Experience, and a Ph. D. in Common Sense. Harry Truman was a Hero. Until the day he died, President Harry Truman had a Clear Conscience.

---

[5] I have hated to give this book any publicity, and I'm happy to report that I could not find it in a library, but on a bargain book counter.

CHAPTER 14

Tenacity of the Japanese

I f there was any question concerning the tenacity of the Japanese in their insane loyalty to the Emperor, it was certainly demonstrated after the surrender was proclaimed by the Emperor and the Japanese leaders. For many years after the official surrender on August 15, 1945, Japanese soldiers held out on many of the outposts of the Pacific War, even though on that particular island, or in that particular locale they were living in isolation. The Bushido, "way of the warrior" of the Japanese required them to fight the Emperor's war to the bitter end and they demonstrated this for many years after the war had ended.

One, Sergeant Shoichi Yokoi, held out for 27 years after the war until 1972. He stated that "Japanese soldiers were told to prefer death to the disgrace of getting captured alive." He stated "I am living for the Emperor for the spirit of Japan."

Many holdouts stayed in Guam's jungles for many years and raided and killed natives and also military personnel on Guam. One of those Americans killed on December 14, 1945 was PFC William C. Patrick Bates, who was killed in an ambush by Japanese on Guam.

Even after this there were hundreds of Japanese still hiding in the jungles and remained a problem constantly until the last one previously referred to, Sergeant Shoichi Yokoi, surrendered. The battle in which PFC Bates was killed involved the Third Battalion of the Third Marines and involved a skirmish on the Asian-Piti Beaches and was some 4 months after the official surrender. Six Japanese were killed and about a dozen captured. Guam, of course, had a dense jungle-type vegetation and was ideal for enabling stragglers to survive for many years, and they did so.

The most Japanese holdouts were naturally in the Philippines the largest of the occupied islands, and between August 20 and October 23, 1945, 218 Japanese were killed and more than 67,000 were captured on Northern Luzon. Then in November there were many more prisoners taken and one mass surrender netted 700 Japanese. As late as February 1946, the estimate of Japanese still in the hills and jungles of the Philippines was 4,000. It was estimated there were as many as 800 on Luzon, and 600 in the Visayan Islands.

The first Tarlac Regiment on Lubang Island near Manila Bay engaged about 30 Japanese, which had been terrorizing the area, on February 22, 1946. The US 86th Division officers accompanying the regiment reported at least 6 Japanese killed. On January 1, 1946, 20 Japanese stragglers wondered into the area of the 345th Graves Registration Company and surrendered. These seemed to be in excellent health.

One of the more unbelievable places in which the Japanese stragglers survived and carried on their undying fight for the Emperor was on the island of Peleliu. On April 21, 1947 about 33 Japanese soldiers came in after Marine patrolling and surrendered their battle flag and sword to Navy Captain Leonard O. Fox. This group was lead by Japanese Lieutenant Ei Yamaguchi.

Peleliu had been captured and declared secure in October, 1944; and the main remaining Japanese garrison in the Palau Islands had surrendered September 2, 1945 but the diehards on Peleliu continued to survive until March of 1947. The renegade commander illustrated the leadership of the Japanese. He shot those who advocated surrender and demanded suicide for those wounded in encounters with Marine patrols.

The Marine garrison on Peleliu had been reinforced and Operation Capitulation was instituted to finalize the cleanup of Peleliu and as previously stated, the remainder finally surrendered to Captain Leonard Fox when Lieutenant Ei Yamaguchi turned over his samurai sword and battle flag and those under his command.

So the brilliant professors who arranged the original Enola Gay exhibit, and those who wrote about how ready the Japanese were to surrender, should have carefully analyzed the Japanese indoctrination with their ancient code and ancient Bushido "way of the warrior", and worship of the Emperor.

Let me add one other important factor in the indisputable chain of facts which show that Japan was not, and would not be, even thinking of surrender. Japanese recruits, home guard, and yes, civilians including children were training with packs of explosives, to throw themselves under tanks and blow themselves up. All ages of Japanese were formed into groups training with old firearms and bamboo spears. They were told that the emperor expected them to resist to the death. Their motto: "One Hundred Million Die Together".

CHAPTER 15

Allegiance to the Emperor and Japan

Lest we get carried away with the supposed "wonderful tenacity" of the Japanese soldier and their "loyalty to the Emperor" and their "spirit of Japan", or what their leaders later referred to as a "special sentiment" of allegiance to their country and to the Emperor; we must continue to trace the mind set of the Japanese soldier also in looking upon humans of all other races and nations as being no more than insects or animals for them to look down upon and treat as rats and to experiment with, and to kill, in the most horrible fashion.

We must look at their mindset wherein other nations military personnel and other nations people could be tortured and killed at the whim of the great dedicated super-loyal Emperor's servant, and that they could perform the most unthinkable sickening experiments with human beings, such as; draining all the blood from a person in an experiment, vivisections of live human beings, and amputations of feet, arms and legs without anesthetics. These great super-loyal people used their doctors at Kyushu University to dissect alive 8 of our United States Airmen in May of 1945.

And we need to analyze the minds that would preserve our United States Airmen in formaldehyde to be studied by anatomy students. We need to look beyond how some present day professorial types (and Lifton and Mitchell) now try to glorify them.

These professors (such as those at the National Air and Space Museum) should give us an analytical opinion about reconciling the Japanese Imperial Army of 1944 with humanity when we know of their murdering allied airmen at Hankow, China in December 1944, who after being shot down and taken prisoner were paraded through the street, ridiculed, beaten and tortured while running a gauntlet, and then saturated with gasoline and burned alive. (Personally sanctioned by the Commander of the 34th Japanese Army.)

Is there any understanding of how the entire military regime from the lowest ranking Japanese soldier to the officers and to the Generals, and straight to the Emperor; condoned the torture and killing of our totally helpless American and Allied prisoners of war?

We need to ram those facts down the throats of these latter day geniuses who propose to denigrate the memory of the Enola Gay. They need to understand the final determination of the leaders in Tokyo to kill all the Allied prisoners at the time of any invasion. The orders given at Taihoku Prison on Formosa stated "whether they are destroyed individually or in groups or however it is done, with mass bombing, poisonous smoke, poisons, drowning, decapitation, or what, dispose of the prisoners as the situation dictates. In any case, it is the aim not to allow the escape of a single one, to annihilate them all and not to leave any traces." This was according to the Japanese Headquarters Journal.

Even after the Emperor directed the surrender, thousands of Allied prisoners of war were executed in final acts of brutality. After the Emperor spoke, the last five downed American Airmen were taken to a military cemetery in Osaka, three were shot and two were beheaded. The same day, hours into the peace, Japanese officers at Fukuoka on Kishua took their samurai swords and chopped 16 Airmen to death. And 12 days after the surrender broadcast, the Japanese on Borneo killed the last 30 of their surviving prisoners. Prisoners of war have never received any reparations nor apologies from the Japanese.

Ralph Levenberg, Head of the Special Projects for the American Defenders of Bataan and Corregidor, was a prisoner of war from April 1942 to August of 1945. He states that they were treated very inhumanely. They were the victims of the most atrocious treatment known to mankind and they were forced into slave labor along with this atrocious treatment.

Again, the Japanese have never acknowledged any wrong doing except some vague statement that they regret their occupation in Asia. They particularly refuse to admit it was aggression and as a matter of fact, they prohibit any history book, or historian, from referring to the China invasion as "aggression."

Has anyone ever read where they stated that the bayoneting of prisoners and torturing and killing thousands on the Bataan Death March was wrong? In this writer's humble opinion there has never been a more humiliating, degrading affront to a nation than the Bataan Death March in which the Japanese soldiers tortured and bayoneted our helpless military personnel, and photographed it, flaunting it for the United States of America and for the world to see.

Bataan Death March

This is the country which is now our "Authority on Peace" and they are now the "World's Conscience on War, Peace and on Barbarism." They are the country that is telling us that the Atomic Bomb was barbarism, that the Atomic Bomb can be equated to the Holocaust.

A real tragedy of the aftermath of World War II and which has haunted us till this day, is that we were so intent on rebuilding Japan, and wanting things to go smoothly with the occupation, that we were totally inept and pitiful in our war crimes prosecution in that we did not fix some blame on Emperor Hirohito, nor did we fix enough blame on others. All of the horrible war criminals, other than a few who were executed, were pardoned very soon after their trials; the last being in about 1958, some 13 years later (compare this to the Nuremburg German trials).

We never took the time to document for posterity those terrible acts which permeated the entire Japanese Pacific War and the entire treatment of occupied people and nations and their entire treatment of Allied and other prisoners of war. We were derelict, totally derelict, in our recording and spotlighting for the ages what occurred during, and prior to, World War II by the Japanese Imperial Army; from Soldier, Sailor and Prison Guard to Generals, Admirals and Yes, the Emperor.

General Hideki Tojo made it clear at his war crimes trial what everyone already knew, that the terrible conduct of the military was with the express approval of Emperor Hirohito.

CHAPTER 16

The Super Holocaust

As I stated before; there is no desire to detract from, or minimize, the terrible German Nazi Holocaust in killing some 6 million (6,000,000) Jews.

But, with that being a Holocaust, how do you designate a Japanese reign of terror for a decade or more in which probably 5 times as many people were executed and with many of these 30 million (30,000,000) or so executions being preceded by torture so diversified as to numb the thoughts of all humanity? For example: throwing a Filipino baby in the air and bayoneting it as it falls, dissecting U.S. Airmen alive, and preserving their remains in formaldehyde, cutting open Chinese while alive, cutting off women's breasts and children's arms while alive.

I think you can call it a Super Holocaust.

Japanese troops used Chinese prisoners of war as targets for bayonet practice during the 1937-1938 "Rape of Nanjing".

Victims raped and killed in Nanjing.

The unimaginable and vile conduct of the Japanese military, both before and during World War II has been verified and documented so often and positively that we know it is true. The specific incidents cited in this chapter will give you only a sample of the vile conduct permeating the entire Japanese military during the decades prior to, and then during, World War II. They are only a part of the Japanese Super Holocaust.

Some of the horror stories in this chapter have been referred to in other chapters, but here I want you to read other verbatim, true accounts. Hopefully, this will further drive the truth of this into your mind.

The Other Holocaust: Nanking Massacre and Unit 731

"The fellow knew that it was over for him, and so he didn't struggle." recalled the old former medical assistant of a Japanese Army unit in China in World War II. "But when I picked up the scalpel, that's when he began screaming. I cut him open from the chest to the stomach and he screamed terribly and his face was all twisted in agony. He made this unimaginable sound, he was screaming so horribly. But then he finally stopped."

The former medical assistant who insisted on anonymity, explained the reason for the vivisection. The Chinese prisoner had been deliberately infected with the plague as part of a research project - the full horror of which is only now emerging. The Japanese Army set up Headquarters of Unit 731 near Harbin, China to develop plague bombs for use in World War II. After infecting him, the researchers decided to cut him open to see what the disease does to

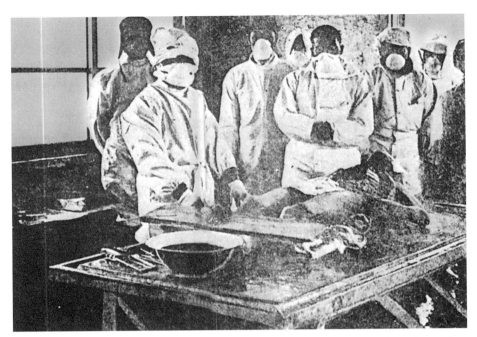

"Medical specialists" of the notorious Unit 731, a Japanese biochemical warfare unit, watched their colleague perform an autopsy on a woman victim and her baby.

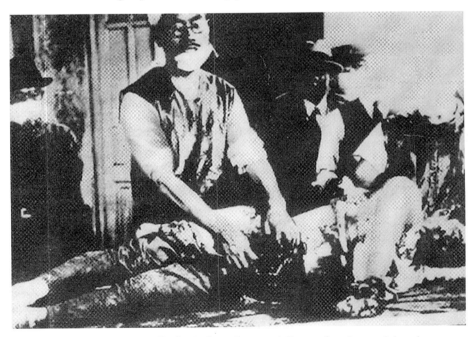

Japanese Army Unit #100. Biological warfare specialist performing a vivisection on a Chinese prisoner.

a man's inside. No anesthetic was used he said, out of concern that it might have an effect on the results.

The research program was one of the great secrets of Japan during and after World War II: a vast project to develop weapons of biological warfare, including plague, anthrax, cholera and a dozen other pathogens. The vivisection was also routinely used for practicing various kinds of surgery says Dr. Ken Yuasa, a former Japanese doctor working in China during the War. First an appendectomy, then an amputation of an arm and finally a tracheotomy. When they finished practicing, they killed the patient with an injection.

Medical researchers also locked up diseased prisoners with healthy ones, to see how readily various ailments would spread. The doctors put others inside a pressure chamber to see how much the body can withstand before the eyes pop from their sockets. To determine the treatment of frostbite, prisoners were taken outside in freezing weather and left with exposed arms, periodically drenched with water, until the frozen arm emitted a sound resembling that which a board gives when it is struck.

The doctors even experimented on a three-day-old baby, measuring the temperature with a needle stuck inside the infant's middle finger to keep it straight to prevent the baby's hand clenching into a fist. Victims were often taken to a proving ground called Anda, where they were tied to stakes and bombarded with test weapons to see how effective the new technologies were. Planes sprayed the zone with a plague culture or dropped bombs with plague-infected fleas to see how many people would die.

The Japanese Army regularly conducted "field tests". Planes

dropped plague-infected fleas over Ningbo in eastern China and over Changde in north-central China, Japanese troops also dropped cholera and typhoid cultures in wells and ponds.

Sheldon H. Harris, a historian at California State University in Northridge and author of this book on Unit 731, *Factories of Death*, estimates that more then 200,000 Chinese were killed in germ warfare field experiments alone. Professor Harris also says plague-infected animals were released as the war was ending and caused outbreaks of the plague that killed at least 30,000 people in the Harbin area from 1946 through 1948.

In what Harris describes as a "Faustian bargain", the research was kept secret after the war in part because the U. S. granted immunity from war crimes prosecution to the Japanese doctors in exchange for their data. Japanese and American documents show that the United States helped cover up the human experimentation. Instead of putting the ringleaders on trial, U.S. gave them stipends.

December 13th 1937, Nanjing fell to the Japanese. Japanese military force immediately, systematically, started murdering Chinese civilians under the "Take all, Kill all, Burn all" military policy. In the next six weeks, the Japanese committed the infamous Nanjing Massacre, or the Rape of Nanjing. The brutalities included shooting, stabbing, cutting open the abdomen, excavating the heart, decapitation, drowning, punching the body and eye with an awl. Thousands of civilians were buried or burn alive, or used as targets for bayonet practice, shot in large groups and thrown into Yangtze River. Soldiers competed in "killing contests" and sent the number of murders back to newspapers in Japan to publish.

These three Japanese soldiers wiped the blood off of their mighty swords during a break from their killing contest.

"I have never been to hell, but there is a hell, it was in this city," reporter for the *Tokyo Times* told of the killing in Nanjing.

Witnessing the atrocities, Reverend John Magee used his camera and recorded the Massacre in a 16mm film. It is believed to be the only documentary about this infamous incident. He was an Episcopal pastor in charge of the so-called Nanjing International Safety Zone created when the Japanese army captured Nanjing in 1937.

Angry at the Japanese atrocities, German diplomat Mr. John Rosen sent a copy of Magee's film to the Nazi government. He also included a long report which claimed that the whole Japanese army was a "Violent Killing Machine". In it, he requested that the film be shown to Hitler. Chinese and Japanese scholars were aware of the film but were unable to locate it. Japanese then said that since there was no proof, the Nanjing Massacre never occurred.

When the German Archive at Potsdam was opened in 1990 after collapsing of the Berlin Wall, the Rosen report surfaced, but the films' whereabouts were still unknown. After a long search, the four rolls of the film and the diaries were finally found in Yale University Library and in the house of Mr. David Magee, Reverend Magee's son. According to Magee's dairy, he could only record a very small part of what he witnessed since he was too busy trying to save lives.

Brackman, a reporter at the Tokyo Trial and author of the book "The Other Nuremberg" commented "The Nanjing Massacre was not the kind of isolated incident common to wars. It was deliberate. It was policy. It was known in Tokyo." Yet it was allowed to continue for over six weeks.

"In terms of measures and cruelty of the genocide, its duration and large numbers of people killed," says professor of history of Southern Illinois University "Neither Hiroshima nor Jewish Holocaust can rival the Nanjing Massacre."[6] The international community estimated that more than 300,000 Chinese were killed, and 20,000 women were raped within six weeks of continuous Massacre.

Yet Japan often said that Japan's aim in World War II was simply to liberate Asia from Western colonialism and later to project themselves as the victims instead of perpetrators of World War II because atomic bombs were dropped on Hiroshima and Nagasaki,

---

[6] The authors of this book disagree with this statement on the Jewish Holocaust.

Women were gang-raped and then killed during the six weeks of "The Rape of Nanjing".

ignoring all the facts that the Nanjing Massacre and infamous Unit 731 were one of the ugliest chapters against humanity in the 20th century. Japan is responsible for the deaths of more than 20 million Chinese, not to mention large numbers of Koreans, Filipinos and other Asian countries. It is a Holocaust committed by Japan in World War II and not yet confessed.

Let me quote a few more specific Nanjing horrors for you.

"The Nanjing egg processing plant, accommodated tens of thousands of refugees. When the Japanese discovered them, they tied them up and killed all of them."

———

"Several thousand wounded and sick POWs, elderly and young refugees were forced into the river by the Japanese who then threw hay sprayed with kerosene on them burning them to death."

Bodies of civilians laid lifeless in the field outside SuZhou, JiangSu Province.

A victim burned to death during "The Rape of Nanjing".

Bodies – murdered victims in Nanjing, 1937.

A Chinese woman disemboweled after being raped and killed.

A Japanese soldier stands over the bodies of Chinese POWs were bayonetted or machine-gunned down near Yuhuatai in Nanjing.

A pile of bodies of children who were killed by the Japanese troops, to be burned at LongWei Shan, TienLien or Iron Ridge – Dragon Tail Mountain in Liaoning Province (Oct. - Nov. 1931).

During the International Tribunal of Nanjing in 1946. Some of the dried bones outside ZhongHua Gate near the military factory were dug up for inspection by members of the Tribunal led by Chief Justice Mr. Shi Mei-Yu.

One of the 30 mass graves in the outskirts of Nanjing – each had more than 10,000 corpses in it – result from "The Rape of Nanjing" (six weeks of killing).

"The disarmed policemen of Nanjing were marched outside the Hamxi Gate and slaughtered."

———

"On December 23, 1937, Japanese drove more than 1,000 elderly, women, and children to the sandbank and buried them alive in a huge pit."

———

"Another occasion they drove six to seven thousand to the sandbank, sprayed kerosene on the crowd and burned them to death. The Japanese stood along side and laughed wildly at the horrifying cries of the victims."

The debate has been smoldering in Japan for the past 40 years. History professor Saburo Ienaga, who has now become for many the living "Conscience of Japan", has launched no less than three highly publicized lawsuits against the Department of Education. Based on his own research, he wrote a high school textbook which included Japan's terrible War crimes: Nanjing Massacre and infamous Unit 731. Time after time again, his manuscripts were sent back from the Education Department. He was asked to delete a reference to the Japanese "aggression" in China and told to use the words "military advance" instead. Regarding the Nanjing massacre, he had to haggle with education officials over the number of Chinese civilians killed. As for the infamous Unit 731, it was made clear that any mention of its existence would quite simply bar the book from publication. Finally Mr. Ienaga got angry and sued the Education Department.

The Ienaga's cases have encouraged testimonies and historical research. In view of the evidence, being unveiled everywhere, the Education Department examiners have had no choice but to relax their criteria even before the final decision of the Supreme Court is handed down. It has now been 12 years since he launched his third lawsuit against the Education Department and there is no telling when the Supreme Court will deliver its final decision. He has lost all his cases before.

"Japan is a very strange country, truth cannot prevail, "Nagase Takashi another former imperial solder, says in a mock incredulous voice, "So I am a citizen of the world and NOT a Japanese." Mr. Nagase is also a devoted crusader for a just cause. He dares to do the unthinkable in Japan. He calls the Japanese royal family the war criminal family, saying the Emperor should either commit harikiri or become a Shinto priest. Hirohito could have stopped the war at any time. And he never took any responsibility.

Japan has successfully brainwashed its own people by glorifying Convicted CLASS A War Criminals As National Heroes and publicly denied the atrocities - Nanjing Massacre and Unit 731. The majority of the Japanese now do not know that Japan had ever invaded another country. Mr. Nagase maintains, "they only know the atomic bomb exploded over Hiroshima and we lost the war." Mr. Nagase believes Japan DESERVED the bombs dropped on Hiroshima and Nagasasi. The atomic bombs immediately stopped the war, saving numerous lives of Japanese, POWs, and civilians in Asian countries.

A further and perhaps, more credible, validation of the atomic bomb decision came from the very man who led the Japanese in the attack on Pearl Harbor. Some 18 years after the war, Mitsuo Fuchida came to the US with a delegation from Japan's Self-Defense Force. The group was observing USAF Operations at MacDill Air Base. Fuchida broke away from the delegation to approach Enola Gay Pilot, Paul Tibbets, who was also in attendance. Speaking bluntly and honestly, Fuchida said to Tibbets,

"You did the right thing. You know the Japanese attitude at the time, how fanatic they were. They'd die for the Emperor. Can you imagine what a slaughter it would be to invade Japan? It would have been terrible. You did the right thing. The Japanese people know more about that than the American public will ever know. Every man, woman, and child would have resisted that invasion with sticks and stones if necessary."

The Japanese constitution bans "land, sea and air forces, as well as other war potential." Yet, because of the wonders of constitutional interpretation, Japan has now built its self-defense into one of the most powerful armies in Asia, supported by the equivalent of US $45 billion military budget, the second or third largest in the world after that of the United States and probably Russia.

The constant reminders of the atrocities of Germany's Nazi regime is now recognized as a major preventive measure against the revival of Nazism in Germany. The annual commemoration of the victims of Hiroshima provides a strong basis for the resistance to the dangers of nuclear wars. To bring attention to the war crimes committed by Japan can prevent the resurgence of militarism anywhere in the world as well.

Listen to Ignatius Ding of the Alliance to Preserve the History of the Sino-Japanese War:

"If Japan wants to play a larger political role in the World or to secure a permanent seat on the UN Security Council, Japan must settle its past. Adopting a "No War Resolution" without a formal apology to the victims during the War, Japan missed again a golden opportunity to reconcile with its neighbors. Denial will not make the past go away. Only facing the truth of history with courage as Germany, can Japan bring the wounds of war a final closure. Until this is done, Japan remains as a country without SOUL."

The Manila Horror Story — More of the Super Holocaust

This true account of events at the time of the fall of Manila to the Allies in 1945, is all supported by numerous eyewitness affidavits.

"Manila has been destroyed. The once proud city of the Far East is dead. Its churches, convents and universities are piles of rubble, bombed and burned beyond recognition. Its civilian population has been raped and burned, starved and murdered, its women mutilated, its babies bayoneted.

The order that brought this about came directly from Tokyo. Reliable evidence based on interrogation of prisoners of war, military personnel, Philippine officials and civilians, and Japanese documents reveal the staggering fact that the sack of Manila and its attendant horrors were not the act of a crazed garrison in a last-ditch, berserk defense, but the coldly planned purpose of the Japanese High Command.

In the first three weeks of February 1945, commencing with the liberation of the Santo Tomas internment camp, the Japanese began to burn and destroy systematically the churches, convents and charitable institutions of Intramuros, the old "Walled City." They destroyed all of its most sacred and historic properties.

They reduced to a rubble heap the fine old Pontifical University of Santo Tomas, the greatest Catholic university in the Orient and the oldest under the American flag. Only the ruined walls were left of the Manila Cathedral, the most beautiful church in the Far East. The Archbishop's Palace, hospitals, convents, schools, libraries were bombed and burned. The cultural monuments that made of Intramuros a miniature Rome have been obliterated.

Outside of Intramuros the Japanese destroyed, with the same cold calculation, Spanish institutions belonging to the Sister of Charity. In Looban Asylum, when the Japanese burned the convent, were more than a thousand refugees, mostly women and children. In Concordia College there were more than 2,000 refugees - babies, orphans and foundlings, sick people, and the insane who had been transferred from the Hospicio de San Jose. Did the Japanese give these helpless people a comparatively merciful death by shooting them? They did not waste their ammunition on these women and children, these sick and insane. They closed the doors with chains, surrounded the building with machine guns to prevent anyone from leaving the premises alive, then set the building on fire.

On February 10, 1945, a squad of Japanese soldiers entered the Red Cross building and proceeded to shoot and bayonet everyone there, including staff doctors, patients, babies, nurses and refugees. Nurses pleaded for the lives of mothers with newborn infants but all were bayoneted or shot. Then the attackers ransacked the building for food and supplies. Modesto Faroian, acting manager of the Philippine Red Cross escaped. Under affidavit he has described the Japanese atrocities.

On February 12 a Japanese officer and 20 soldiers forced their way into La Salle College where 70 people were living, including 30 women and young girls, children, 15 brothers and a priest, and the adult men of four families. All the inmates were shot, attacked with sabers, or bayoneted. Many who did not die during the attack, bled to death. The attackers attempted to violate young girls while they were dying from bullet wounds and bayonet slashes. The chapel was set afire and only 10 of the victims survived. The Father Superior, who escaped, described the massacre under affidavit.

On February 23, 50 bodies were discovered in a 12-by-15-foot room in Fort Santiago. The bodies, riddled with bullets, the hands tied behind their backs, were shrunken and gave the appearance of malnutrition and near-starvation. These bodies were piled in layers, several feet high. In another room were eight bodies in the same condition.

On the same day, 30 bodies were found in a small stone building 15 feet square. The bodies were all burned or scorched. A Filipino, who had been bayoneted by the Japanese but had survived and escaped directed an American sergeant to the chamber of death. He was one of 58 tubercular patients who had been removed from a hospital and brought to the area. They were left without food or water. Whenever the patients asked for water or food they were bayoneted and thrown into the building of the dead.

On February 24 a heap of 250 to 300 bodies were found in a 15-

by-18-foot dungeon, which was barred and closed by steel doors. The dungeon was without every indication these people had died of starvation. Positions of the bodies showed they had struggled desperately to escape. American officers who opened the doors attested that the stench was like a blast.

Even thought the Spanish flag was prominently displayed at the Spanish Consulate, the Japanese torched the building and more than 50 people were burned alive or killed with bayonets in the garden. The Casino Espanol and the library were burned. The House of the Auxilio Social and the Patronato Escobar Espanol were burned. It is estimated that 90 percent of the Spanish property in Manila was destroyed.

The provinces fared no better. On February 1, 1945, the Japanese dynamited the sugar central "El Real" in Calamba, belonging to the Dominican Order. In Calamba, 5,000 men, women and children were killed and the town was completely destroyed by fire. Five priests, tied and about to be killed, were saved and related under affidavit their experience.

In Intramuros most of the Spanish priests and brothers were conducted by the military police to two shelters in front of the Cathedral. When they were penned in the shelters, the Japanese soldiers threw hand grenades among them, then covered the entrances to the shelters with gasoline drums and earth - burying them alive. Out of 13 Augustinian priests, only two were saved. Franciscan, Capuchin and Recollect priests were killed in the same way. Outside Intramuros 15 Paulist and three Capuchin priests were killed.

Dr. Walter K. Frankel, 55 years old, a surgeon, urologist, lecturer on history of medicine in the College of Medicine of the University of the Philippines, and 19 other, including men, women and children, were herded into a room and surrounded by gasoline-saturated furniture that was set on fire. Those who tried to escape were shot. Frankel, his sister, and one other person survived. Frankel's story with signed affidavit, described these tortures.

On February 7, on the southeast corner of Juan Luna and Moriones streets, 49 mutilated bodies were found scattered on the grass, on the pavement, and in ditches of water. Approximately one-third were babies or young children and about one-third were women. Most of the bodies were found with hands tied behind their backs. On the same day the bodies of 115 men, women and children were found on the grounds of the Dy-Pac Lumber Co. near the railroad station. The Japanese had shot and bayoneted these people and pushed their bodies into the ditches. Many adults and some older children were tied, while very small children had been killed without having been tied. The children were from 2 to 10 years old. Some of the women were pregnant.

Enemy documents about the massacre include a diary entry recording the death of 1,000 civilians by burning, a battalion order giving instructions for the disposal of civilians by burning and an order instructing that all people on that battlefield, with the exception of Japanese, are to be killed.

At the Campos residence on Taft Avenue, the bodies of 45 women were found, cruelly mutilated, with evidence of assault apparent. In this group were several children, all of whom had been bayoneted.

The individual atrocities, as told by the survivors were countless

Victims of Japanese atrocities were usually the most vulnerable ones. Women and children in Chinese cities and countrysides.

and barbarous. Women were slashed with sabers, their breasts cut off, their genitals pierced with bayonets; children were cut and stabbed with sabers and bayonets. Men, trying to save their belongings from burning homes, were burned with flame-throwers and forced back into the burning buildings. Few escaped alive. An affidavit made by Medical Officer John H. Amnesse lists such wounds as teen-aged girls with both nipples amputated and bayonet wounds in the chest and abdomen, a 10-year-old girl and a two-year-old-boy with arms amputated, children under five suffering severe burns and stab wounds. Further evidence of atrocities committed can be found in any of the civilian hospitals in the area."

One of the last occurrences cited in an affidavit about Philippine atrocities: "As Diomisio fled he saw a Japanese soldier pick a baby up, throw it into the air and catch it with a fixed bayonet."

The above accounts were all supported by affidavits.

We repeat one horrid act, to continue to make you want to be sensitive to Japanese feelings about Hiroshima: "At Kyushu University near Fukuoka, Japan, eight U.S. airmen were dissected alive in May of 1945 and their remains preserved in formaldehyde.

Some authors write about the 4th Hague Convention of 1907, Geneva Convention and various war related conventions and treaties which bound the Japanese to certain humane conduct in wartime. To analyze the Japanese Imperial Army in this manner is a waste of time. They should have been bound by being human (which they were not at the time) not to carry out the atrocities they perpetrated in China, Asia and the Pacific.

CHAPTER 17

Super Holocaust: All Japanese Knew

Should there be any doubt that the entire Japanese populace, the Emperor, the Military Leaders and the entire nation, supported the Japanese Imperial Army in all its atrocious conduct, that thought is dispelled in the recorded black and white print of the newspapers of Japan.

During the Nanking Massacre two officers of the Katagiri unit, Sub-lieutenant Toshiaki Mukai and Sub-lieutenant Takeshi Noda entered into a race to kill 100 Chinese people near the Purple Mountain outside of Nanking.

When they met to compare their gruesome progress, Noda had 105, and Mukai had 106. They are quoted as laughing heartily about this, but found it impossible to determine which had passed

Front page headline news in *The Tokyo Daily* praising the courage of two Japanese Officers, Sub-lieutenant Toshiaki Mukai and Sub-lieutenant Takeshi Noda. They were competing in a killing contest; Noda had 105 and Mukai 106.

the 100 mark first, so they decided to extend the goal to another 50.

Both thought the contest was fun and a good thing that both men had gone over 100 without knowing the other had done so.

Mukai's blade had been damaged, as he explained, by cutting a Chinese in half, helmut and all.

The reader must realize that this was not a military battlefield contest, and while it was described in Japan as a "Killing Contest", that is a total misnomer. It was a "Slaughter Contest" as they were only slaughtering defenseless women, children, elderly and unarmed prisoners.

An account of this nauseating contest was published by the *Nichi Nichi Shimbun* in Tokyo on December 13, 1937. A similar story was published in the *Tokyo Daily* praising the courage of these two Japanese officers.

Gunkichi Tanaka, another brave warrior, at about the same time was credited with killing more than 300 P.O.W.s and civilians in a southwest suburb of Nanking in December, 1937.

While we do not know if he was given the same "hero's" publicity in the news media, we do know he received enough publicity to be tried as a war criminal.

The denials of the atrocities fade away in the light of the recorded news stories in Japan.

These recorded news stories in Japan prove that the atrocities of the Japanese Military cannot be brushed aside with the comment that all armies have some rogue soldiers and rogue units.

This was a rogue military leading straight to the Emperor.

CHAPTER 18

The Super Holocaust in Pictures

The pictures in this Chapter along with each caption, have been furnished to us by the "Alliance for Preserving the Truth of the Sino-Japanese War." This organization is largely composed of Chinese-Americans who have done extensive research on the conduct of the Japanese Imperial Army while in China.

These pictures vividly, though only in a small way, show the atrocities numbering above thirty million (30,000,000) committed by the Japanese Imperial Army while in China. Add to this the identical conduct in the Philippines and throughout Southeast Asia and you might (with great imagination) visualize the Super Holocaust spread out from 1931 through 1945.

Chinese POW being used as a "live target" in bayonet practice, XyZhou (near Nanking), June 1928.

A grinning Japanese officer chopping off the head of an old Chinese farmer.

Chinese POW used for bayonet practice as "live target" by Japanese solders, XyZhon June 1928 (near Nanking).

This photo is stamped with "Not permitted to release" by the military, shows the brutal treatment of the Chinese POWs by the Japanese Army.

Japanese troops using live POWs for bayonet practice.

Beheading a POW in Nanjing, December 1937.

A young Chinese boy selling candies was caught with 30 cents in his pocket. The money was issued by the retreating Chinese government. Possession of such currency in the occupied territory as considered a crime by the Japanese military. He was tied to a tree on 2nd Blvd. in Jinan, Shandong and beheaded.

A Japanese military officer beheading a POW.

Japanese troops displayed heads of their prisoners to demonstrate their "unchallenge-able authority" in China.

A grinning
Japanese officer
beheading a
civilian.

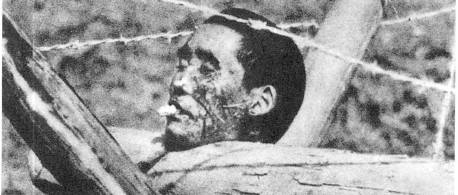

A head displayed in public after a civilian was beheaded.

"An Educational Special" for new Japanese recruits – the killing of POWs and civilians.

The germ warfare factory set up by Japanese Army Unit #100 at MenJia Tuen, outside of Changchun in Manchuria. From early 1930s through 1945, at least five different germ bombs containing contagious diseases were mass produced each year.

After the Japanese troops left Heng Yang City of Hunan Province in 1945, these dried bones and skeletons were discovered among several mass graves. The Chinese soldiers and civilians in the city had shared the same fate after the 47 days of siege of Heng Yang in 1938

August 4, '95

Dear M/s. M. Nakagawa:

It' my pleasure that I found the right person to send these photos, because I always felt sorry for chinese people, and Japanese Imperial Army was so cruel unneccesarily, they were nothing but murderers. I found two pictures, very Old. my descriptions about the pictures were not right, or I maybe have another one; I couldn't find it today.

Sincerely,

The family of a deceased WWI veteran of the Japanese Imperial Army sent this letter and 2 pictures to the Global Alliance from Chino, CA after they have seen the photo exhibit of Japanese atrocities in Los Angeles, CA in 1995. A Japanese American Newspaper helped forward them to the Alliance. (signature on file)

CHAPTER 19

What if the Japanese Had the Atomic Bomb First?

It is not very difficult to imagine the end result of World War II if the Japanese had developed the Atomic Bomb.

There is no question that all major participants in World War II were interested in a "super" bomb of some kind and the Japanese had certainly made progress and had hope to have a "super" bomb.

Can you imagine a country that had bombed Pearl Harbor without any notice and a country that had invaded China all the South Pacific Islands, the Philippines, Malaysia, Singapore and Indo-China would have hesitated to use the bomb on us?

Which city would have been the first target, Los Angeles? San Francisco? Seattle? Which of these would have been wiped off the map with far more deaths than the two cities we selected.

And a little beyond the use of the bomb on us, how would we have been treated "post-war" compared to our rehabilitation of the Japanese people and the Japanese society?

Compare that with the treatment of the Chinese people and the Philippine people after they were conquered, the Koreans after they were occupied (with the Koreans ability to resist being nil; it could hardly be called conquering; they were simply taken over). You can imagine the atrocities in our country when you magnify the ones that occurred in the Philippines, and in all of the other occupied islands and countries in the far east.

Just meditate a moment about the Nanjing Massacre, the Singapore hospital massacres, the Hong Kong massacres, the Philippine hospital and Manila massacres, the Bataan Death March, and transfer that to California.

The atrocities there were unbelievable and we can only imagine what would have occurred had the bomb been used by the Japanese and our people subjected to their occupation.

Doesn't take a strong imagination to multiply what occurred in the Philippines by a hundred or a thousand and realize what would have occurred with us in the United States of America, had the Japanese developed the Bomb and subjected our people to a Nanking-like occupation.

Western Imperialism — A Feeble Excuse

The principal theme of the Japanese as the reason for their expansion into Asia and the Pacific sphere was that they were preventing Western Imperialism.

When the Japanese occupied Indo-China in September of 1940, long before Pearl Harbor, I am sure everyone in Indo-China understood that it was only to prevent Western Colonialism, and when the Japanese also attacked the Philippines, Singapore, Hong Kong and Malaysia at about the same time as Pearl Harbor, we must be sure that those people also understood that they were being protected from 'Western Colonialism', and when in January, Indonesia was captured, I am sure they welcomed the protection from Western Imperialism and then in March of 1942, Burma would, of course, be delighted to be conquered by the Japanese, and also be protected from Western Colonialism.

And of course, all of the South Pacific, including the Solomon Islands, were delighted to be occupied by the bloody force of the Japanese. Certainly only to protect them.

And one would need to talk to the Aussies, to be assured that everyone in Australia was looking forward to Australia being invaded and protected from the Imperialistic British and their colonialism.

CHAPTER 20

Commentary

Now admittedly most of the previous portions of this book are sprinkled with recrimination or vituperative comments about the Japanese, or those who trumpet or espouse the line that the Japanese were pure victims of the Bomb and Western Colonialism. You must be assured that this occasional hint of sarcasm is solely to point out that the Japanese are in no position to criticize the use of The Bomb and that, in their criticism of The Bomb, it is the Japanese purpose to divert the populace of the world from the only narrow issue involved in ordering the dropping of the Bomb. That narrow issue was: Would the use of the Atomic Bomb save Allied lives; and secondarily, would it save Japanese lives.

There are those who proclaim the right of historians to use "changing times" to write what they say "true history" is and that those who lived through the war always think of Pearl Harbor when use of the Atomic Bomb is mentioned. They say that Veterans and people who lived through the War are incapable of objectively deciding whether the Bomb was correct.

After Congressional hearings on the proposed Enola Gay exhibit in the National Air and Space Museum, the Director of the National coordinating Committee for the Promotion of History noted in her summary that "the real losers in this hearing was history." She emphasized "**None of the Senators** seemed to really understand that history is not static but is constantly being refined, as both the questions that are asked and the primary sources that are available allow a more comprehensive and accurate view of the past to emerge."

Now when I read this over and over it just seems to this country Judge that this is what Harwit, his infallible over-educated panel of professors, and Gar Alperovitz, Robert Lifton and Greg Mitchell are all claiming the right to do. Revise history **as they see it**.

What?? History not static!!!

History certainly can be revised when new facts are discovered. But, my friends, no new facts have been discovered to alter President Harry Truman's decision on the Bomb.

Do not tell me for a minute that a statement in the proposed Enola Gay Exhibit, and I quote: " For the Japanese the war in the Pacific was a war to protect his unique culture and homeland. For the Americans this was a war of vengeance", is a recently discovered fact.

Let this soak in. This is not a historical fact. It is the prattling of a revisionist historian. History did not lose anything by not having this in an exhibit. By whose definition is this "true history"?

CHAPTER 21

Yasukuni Shrine

The Yasukuni Shrine is a shrine at the northern edge of the Imperial Palace in Tokyo. The American people, in considering how the Japanese feel about history and the war, should know about the Yasukuni Shrine. This shrine is a national shrine. The Japanese built it to make heroes of all Japanese who fought for Japan and died in all their wars including World War II. They are all considered kami, or gods, if they served in their military, fought for Japan and died, no matter how brutal or savage their conduct had been.

Yasukuni Shrine also includes all those who tortured and killed American service men in the Bataan Death March in the Philippines. It includes as Kami (god) all of the soldiers who brutalized and murdered the 300,000 Chinese in the 'Rape of Nanjing' massacre. Also included as Kami, are all of the soldiers who rampaged across China and Asia and participated in killing the 30,000,000 Chinese during the occupation of a great portion of China before and during World

War II, in the most brutal of all military occupations.

It includes all those soldiers from the infamous Unit 731 in China who injected Chinese with plague, experimented with deadly germ and biological tests on Chinese, and dissected Chinese alive (Oh, you heroes).

It includes kamikaze pilots who killed American Navy personnel by diving planes into their ship whether it was a military ship or a hospital ship, and it therefore includes those who killed nurses with kamikaze attacks during World War II. A plaque to the Kamikaze pilots declares "the suicide operators, incomparable in their tragic bravery, struck terror in their foes and engulfed the entire country in tears of gratitude for their outstanding loyalty and selfless service". When I read or think about these Emperor-loyal Kamikaze zealots dying for the Emperor, I always remember General George Patton's admonition to his troops; that in War "It's not your mission to die for your country, but to make some other bastard die for his."

Further spitting in our face (figuratively) about World War II, Japanese veterans stand outside this Japanese shrine and hand out brochures stating that "Japan's army in World War II fought in a noble effort to free Asia from white colonialism."

The central hall of the Yasukuni Shrine museum contains such exhibits as the 40 foot kai-ten human suicide torpedo and the ohka, or cherry blossom plane, a light plane used for kamikaze attacks.

In short, any person who served in the military, no matter how brutal they were, becomes a Kami, or god, upon death in combat.

Well, really you did not have to die in combat for the Emperor, to be enshrined at Yasukuni. The most prominent War Criminal of Japan who was executed, is enshrined there as a hero. Wartime Prime Minister Hideki Tojo, and all the other war criminals who were convicted are enshrined there. We should mention here again, what a terrible job we did in punishing war criminals in Japan, only a pitiful few.

The name of the shrine "Yasukuni" means "peaceful country". The shrine is supposed to celebrate, "the soldiers who, since 1850 sacrificed their lives so Japan could enjoy peace today.[7]"

This shrine is spitting in the face of the United States of America and this from a people who have criticism for our trying to put a historical exhibit concerning the Enola Gay in our Smithsonian Institute. How dare they do this! How dare any 'wild mindless American' support them by distorting history in the proposed Enola Gay exhibit. All this while we are trying, for some 50 years, to be delicate and understanding, and in no manner wanting to offend the Japanese in the way we treat the Pacific War, and allowing them to use the Atomic Bomb to place guilt on us and make us the aggressors, and make the Japanese people the victims. This has culminated in elaborate speeches condemning Americans as barbaric, some 50 years after the war.

To the credit of the Japanese people, the best information available indicates that a majority of the Japanese want the truth about the war and the atrocities to be told, and do not support this misleading, flawed shrine. It is a shame that the rabid self-proclaimed patriotic few, are able to be loud and dominant enough to prevail on

---

[7] Many citizens of the United States of America and our Allies sacrificed their lives so that Japan could enjoy peace today.

this distorted historic theme.

Compare the vile insulting nature of the Yasukuni Shrine to our little pitiful attempt at a historic stamp.

In December 1994 the U.S. Postal Service was completing a set of ten commemorative stamps to mark the 50th Anniversary of the end of the war. The series was entitled "World War II - 1945: victory at Last" and the last stamp bore a picture of an atomic mushroom cloud and an inscription "Atomic bombs hasten war's end, August 1945." Totally historic. Totally correct. Well, what do you know! It offended the Japanese and gave them a chance to cry again about the bomb. After they, a few of our idiots, and President Clinton objected to the 'insensitivity' of the stamp and the White House put pressure on the Postal Service to redo the design, the stamp was replaced by one with President Truman announcing the end of the war.

If you read this book and other valid accounts of the Japanese, you know that **"insensitive"** is a word Japanese should never dare to use to us, or the World.

Many blamed the Postal Service for being spineless, but the real gutless conduct was by President Clinton and the White House staff in not supporting the Postal Service, and saying that the Stamp was a fact we were within our historical right to proclaim. As a matter of fact it was not insensitive, it was fact. Follow their reasoning and we can't even celebrate the end of the war.

As a matter of fact, we cannot properly celebrate the end of the war. We're supposed to (in deference to Japanese feelings) call it V-P Day instead of V-J Day. We don't know who the hell else we were fighting in the Pacific.

CHAPTER 22

The 10 Most Awful Things That Should Never Happen Again

The pacifists, revisionists, "politically correct" and "distortionists of history" all have in their writings the theme, or hope, that the Atomic Bombings never occur again.

Using things we know occurred during and prior to World War II, let's put our perspective on a list of the "The 10 Most Awful Things" which all the World would hope should never happen again.

1. Killing millions (probably 30,000,000 Chinese, 1,500,000 Filipinos and 1,000,000 in other countries) of people while occupying their country.

2. Jewish Holocaust - 6,000,000 Jews massacred.

3. Killing of prisoners as a part of an "Impending Defeat Plan", Torturing and killing prisoners on a Bataan Type Death March, and torturing and killing all downed airmen, as in Japan.

4. Sneak attack on another unsuspecting country (such as Pearl Harbor).

5. Killing of civilians as a part of an "Impending Defeat Plan", as in The Philippines.

6. Dissecting of humans as a military experiment; particularly while they are still alive.

7. Biological disease or germ warfare experiments on humans.

8. Bayonet practice on live humans, babies and children included, to toughen soldiers for killing.

9. Teaching kamikaze practices; and that suicide, in the face of capture, is honorable. Teaching millions of civilians; men, women and children that they must die for an Emperor, who is God.

10. Use of an Atomic Bomb (unless, of course, it is to save millions of lives).

CHAPTER 23

The Japanese Today — No Understanding of the War

Tragically it is apparent that 50 years later Japanese citizens, especially the younger generation, have no true perspective of World War II. The Japanese citizen does not know about the atrocities that occurred during World War II. The average Japanese has no true idea of the occurrences in Korea. The average Japanese does not know the Asian dominance which the Japanese sought, the totally cruel, conquering type war carried on in China and in Indo-China. The average Japanese is not aware of the false claims made by the Japanese historians that they were protecting their homeland, instead of conquering and occupying islands and other nations which have never been any threat to Japan, or any other country. The average

Japanese is not aware of the Japanese idea of total domination of the Pacific area. The average Japanese does not understand that the Japanese sought to conquer all of China, Southeast Asia and the entire Pacific. Nor are they aware of the Super Holocaust during all of these occupations. It is a shame that the Japanese people are not given the opportunity to appreciate and understand history.

It is more of a shame that they do not appreciate the contribution of the United States of America to their current political processes. Never in the history of mankind has any nation occupied another nation with such benevolent care and with such compassion in rebuilding a completely destroyed economy. We have certainly been the friend of the Japanese. This book is not designed to bash Japan and is not designed to bash the Japanese people or to create a gap between our society or effect our friendship. It is to let you know that under no circumstances should we be criticized about ending the war. Think about this: when has any occupying country ever paid for the rehabilitation of a nation that has attacked them? The United States of America has never started a war, never taken reparations from any country. Can you imagine the reparations to which the United States of America would be entitled if as a conquering nation, we had assessed reparations against Japan for the cost of the Pacific portions of World War II? Japan would never have recovered economically to this day.

Japanese generations since World War II should have been given access to all of the true history of Japan's expansion through out China, Asia and the entire Pacific, and then they would know not to allow the Mayor of Nagasaki, or any other public official to lambaste the United States of America and even hint that it was barbaric conduct, which it wasn't.

We have been a friend of the Japanese, we are now friends of the Japanese. The Japanese have been allowed to promote their economy, at our expense, by business here in the United States of America.

Certainly my own experience is that we have a fine company here in my home town of Cedartown, Georgia; Kimoto Tech; which has wonderful people both as owners and as employees from Japan who have been excellent local citizens who are our friends, and we consider them strong friends. As a matter of fact, Ujihito Kimoto, the founder and owner of the company, fought in the Pacific as a Japanese soldier. He was a friend of mine and we discussed the war historically. No animosity whatsoever on his part, or mine. He was an excellent person. Never any criticism on his part.

The Kimoto family in short is a delightful and excellent family and part of the community here in my home town of Cedartown, Georgia. They, and their Japanese employees, and their entire organization, which has had much contact here in Cedartown, know that we harbor no ill will against them for anything concerning World War II, which is over.

We would only appreciate that they and their children understand, and the Japanese history disclose, the true history of the Japanese expansion, the entire occupation of the Pacific Islands, much of China and Asia, and their dream to capture the rest of the Pacific. And also their aim to conquer Australia, the prevention of which was the first object of our maneuvers during the early stages of World War II.

We only want their history books and their comments and statements from their leaders to reflect the true history of the war leading up to the Atomic Bomb.

In March of 1995, Nagasaki's Mayor, Hitoshi Motoshima called nuclear bombing of Japan the "moral equivalent of the holocaust." This should never go unanswered by our leaders and by the world, in loud, clear, unequivocal terms. The Japanese should understand what Barbaric is. It is not bombing for the purpose of ending a war. Saving millions of lives both military and civilian, is not barbaric. Barbaric is cruelly killing 300,000 people for no reason other than being savage and to show that it can be done, as in Nanking.

Barbaric is killing people to conquer small defenseless countries and islands.

Barbaric is negated by the conduct of the American forces and the American people after World War II.

Instead of ever mentioning the word barbaric to future Japanese generations, thanks to the United States of America should be included in every history book, for their compassion after the war.

Never in the history of civilization has any country been more benevolent to a conquered people (both in Europe and particularly in Japan) than the United States of America was in helping them to rebuild their economy to world power economic status.

In June of 1997, German Chancellor Helmut Kohl thanked the United States of America for the Marshall Plan which saved Germans (and other Europeans) from starving and helped their economies to recover. We did more than that for the Japanese and where has there ever been a word of thanks about it.

Our economy to this day has suffered because of our billions of dollars paid to win a war that we should never have been in.

Barbarism is the Holocaust. The Jewish Holocaust by Nazi Germany of course is Barbarism to its nth degree and beyond.

Barbarism is engulfing a whole nation, such as China and Korea and to continually rape the women of the country. Subjecting the women of the country to the most horrible and enslaved lives imaginable. Uprooting people from their family and their homes. Controlling the children. Killing the population that was in any manner opposed to the occupation of their country by the Japanese. That is barbarism. Barbarism is the Japanese Super Holocaust.

Listen carefully, those of you who speak of "barbaric." The practice of cannibalism, the eating of the humans they killed, by the Japanese military, was real barbarism.

Barbarism is torturing and killing people for no other purpose than the sadistic gratification of the minds of the conqueror.

Killing in self defense has never been and never shall be barbarism. Killing to save ones own life is self defense, and certainly no less self-defense is the killing of some 190,000 people at the height of a war to save millions of lives on both sides. In no manner can that be considered barbaric.

In summary, the Japanese have no standing[8] in the 'Forum of World Opinion' to criticize the Atomic Bomb, or anything we did to end the war.

SHUT UP ABOUT THE BOMB.

---

[8] In law "standing" is the right of a person or group to complain about an occurrence. The right to complain can be forfeited.

Acknowledgements

I strongly recommend you read these other books and materials on the Japanese Empire prior to and during World War II:

Knights of Bushido, by Edward Russell

> (Horror stories of Japanese atrocities)

Factories of Death, by Sheldon H. Harris

> (Horror stories of Japanese atrocities)

The Last Great Victory, by Stanley Weintranb

> (End of World War II)

Prisoners of the Japanese, by Gavan Daw

> (Horror stories of Japanese atrocities)

Where the Buck Stops, writings of Harry S. Truman, edited by Margaret Truman

The Rape of Nanking, by Iris Chang

> (A thoroughly researched account of Japanese atrocities in Nanking)

You should also try to keep up with the following projects and organizations through the internet or News Media, or just writing to them.

Karen Parker, Juris Doctor, Diploma

(International Law of Human Rights) Strasbourg, who practices in International, Human Rights and Humanitarian (armed conflict) Law. She is an expert in Human Rights Law and particularly as it applies to the "jugun ianfu" comfort women enslaved by the Japanese Imperial Army during World War II. She, most properly, designates them as War-Rape Victims, they being women and girls as young as 12 years of age taken from their homes in Korea, China, Dutch East Indies, Taiwan, Malaysia, Burma and the Philippines. Then distributed like cattle to service the Japanese Imperial Army.

There is presently a lawsuit in Japanese Courts for the few survivors of this horrid rape. The Japanese courts have, predictably, granted no relief to these victims because of the Japanese government's position that there was no project of this kind, and, that even if there was, it has been settled by previous treaties.

It may be that the only way to get the Japanese attention on this project and others is a boycott of Japanese products, mainly cars; as recommended by the Global Alliance for the Preservation of the History of World War II in Asia. The Global Alliance is composed of about 30 organizations interested in all phases of the atrocious history of the Japanese which have been almost obliterated since World War II. One of their member groups is:

Alliance for Preserving The History of the Sino-Japanese War
P. O. Box 2066, Cupertino, Calif. 95015
Attn: Mr. Ignatius Ding

This alliance recently sponsored an "International Conference on Japanese Responsibility of World War II Atrocities" at Stanford University, Palo Alto, California, December 6 - December 8, 1996.

While I became more angry as I continued to research and compile this book, there were some heart-warming discoveries. Dr. Eisuke Matsui, Japanese Radiologist appeared at the Stanford University Conference avowing that Japan needed to let their younger generation and all of Japan know about the historical past of the germ attacks by the Japanese and for his country to acknowledge the past. (I have stated elsewhere that every indication is that the majority of Japanese want the historical truth to be known.)

Also encouraging is that "The Japan Times" a Japanese newspaper is writing some about the Japanese Imperial Army and its past.

It was good to learn also that a group of Japanese attorneys had investigated the germ warfare atrocities and were preparing to file a lawsuit in Tokyo District Court for victims of the germ warfare in China in mid-1997.

Kinoue Tokudome, a Japanese woman, has done considerable research and writing on the true history of the Sino-Japanese War and has attempted to present an enlightened viewpoint to the Japanese people with a book and many articles published in Japan.

Center for Internee Rights

6060 La Gorce Drive, Miami, Florida 33140-2117

Phone: (305) 864-2558 Fax: (305) 861-8550

Gilbert Hair, Executive Director

They represent both military and civilian persons imprisoned by the Japanese during WWII.

They are pursuing a petition to pass what was HCR 126 concerning the maltreatment of U.S. military and civilian prisoners of war during WWII.

They are fighting Historical Revisionism, and are trying to get all Pacific WWII documents declassified, the same as previously done for European documents.

American Defenders of Bataan and Corregidor. This organization has researched and consulted on Japanese biochemical warfare during the war. The Director and National Legislative Liaison is Gregory Rodriguez. His father was a survivor of the Bataan Death March and a survivor of the more horrible (if that is possible) Unit 731 germ warfare lab in Mukden, Manchuria. His father passed away in 1996.

Another very admirable organization which should be applauded is the: **The Center for Research and Documentation on Japan's War Responsibility.** This organization on March 31, 1994 filed its first report on the Issue of Japan's Military Comfort Women. I do not want to detract in any way from this brave group, but you should note that this report was over 48 years after the end of World War II. It has taken that long for responsible Japanese to speak out without fear for their lives. You can contact this organization at:

Osaka Office: 2-6-4-518 Shiokusa

Naniwa-Ku, Osaka 556, Japan

Telephone: 06-562-7740

Fax: 06-562-5272.

All of these groups can use your moral, personal, and financial support.

In Gratitude

Many people need to be thanked for helping with this book, beginning with my good friend **Doug Elliott**, who very diligently searched the internet for much material I needed.

Brenda Dempsey, in her spare time, did a great job typing (and retyping) all of the book.

Dick Campbell, of Albuquerque, NM, helped obtain pictures of the mushroom cloud, courtesy of the National Atomic Museum

Senator San Nunn was very helpful.

Carol Leadenham of the Hoover Institution, Stanford University was very gracious in guiding me through some research at the Institute.

Dan Monaco, an attorney and friend, who is a Stanford Graduate, guided me around Palo Alto.

Raul Goco, at the time Solicitor General of the Philippines, helped me with some good material.

Karen Parker, an expert on the "Comfort Women", provided me with some excellent material.

Alex Albert in Senator Paul Coverdell's office helped me get in touch with General Tibbets about the project.

Johnson Printing Company in Cedartown, GA. a big help.

Bob Steed, my good friend and author, was most helpful.

Dick Parker, a Cedartown friend and publisher of "Looking Glass Books," has been a great help.

Sandra Machan and **Debbie Forrister** of the Cedartown, GA library have been exceedingly helpful.

Alex Hawkins, this good friend, ex-NFL player, and great humourous author gave me much encouragement.

Last but not least, members of the **"Alliance for Preserving the Truth of the Sino-Japanese War"** have worked with me during the entire book project. **Ignatius Ding** has worked with me constantly. **Betty Yuan** has given me tremendous support. **Kansen Chu**, the present Chairperson of the Alliance, and his wife, **Daisy Chu**, along with **Eugene L. Wei, Victor Yung, Tony Chang** (*Sing Tao Daily*), **Cathy Tsang** (a founding Vice-President of the Alliance) and other members of the Alliance, honored me with a great informative luncheon (true history lesson) at the Ocean Harbor Restaurant, San Jose, CA. Kansen and Daisy, owners of the restaurant, provided one of the best gourmet meals I have ever enjoyed.

Many thanks go to **Brigadier General Paul W. Tibbets** for our many discussions concerning the use of the Bomb and the revisionists and how to answer them. Everyone should read his revised book, Flight of the Enola Gay.

Deepest thanks go to **General Ray Davis** for joining me in this book and aiding greatly in its credibility.

When I was asked by a friend about the writing of the book I told him, "With a Four Star General and one lowly Marine Major involved, who did you think was going to do the work?"

Judge Dan Winn (Scrivener)
Senior Judge
Superior Courts of Georgia

Judge Winn fought with the U. S. Marine Air Corps. in WWII and received the Distinguished Flying Cross and Air Medal.

Index